DALEY

·THE LAST TEN YEARS·

Daley proudly displaying his newly awarded M.B.E. in 1982

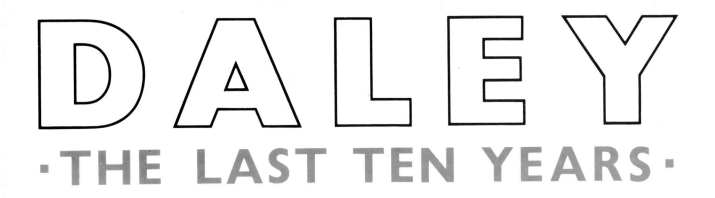

DALEY
·THE LAST TEN YEARS·

DALEY THOMPSON with NEIL WILSON
Photographs by STEVE POWELL

WILLOW BOOKS
Collins
8 Grafton Street, London W1
1986

Willow Books
William Collins Sons & Co Ltd
London • Glasgow • Sydney • Auckland
Toronto • Johannesburg

First published 1986
© Daley Thompson 1986

British Library Cataloguing in Publication Data
Thompson, Daley
 Daley: the last 10 years.   1. Thompson, Daley
 2. Athletes — Great Britain — Biography I. Title
 II. Wilson, Neil, 1944— 796.4'2'0924   GV697.T4/

ISBN 0 00 218229 7

Design by Signal Communications

Printed and bound in Great Britain by
William Collins Sons & Co Ltd, Glasgow

CONTENTS

CHAPTER ONE 1984

Los Angeles Memorial Coliseum, Thursday, August 9, 1984. The Olympic decathlon, discus, third round. To throw: Daley Thompson, of Great Britain, the Olympic champion. He leads the competition by 108 points after six of the ten events from Jurgen Hingsen, of West Germany, the world record holder.

Hingsen has completed his three throws. His longest has scored him 886 points, the best of his life. Thompson's two throws have landed short, the best of them worth only 710 points. Unless he improves with his last he will lose his lead to Hingsen for the first time in their seven competitions. Thompson's future place in Olympic history may hang on the next explosive second, on no more than a turn in the discus circle.

Thompson knows that it is bad for everything to be resting on a third throw but his confidence is high. He chats to the American John Crist, a training partner throughout the year he spent preparing in California. 'Just remember how well you've always thrown when it counts,' Crist says. Thompson nods. He cannot see a problem.

His turn. He walks to the circle. Suddenly he feels different. Hairs on his arms and legs and the back of his neck are standing on end. He cannot recall it happening before. And everything seems

> 66 Looking back over my sporting career it may sound strange to admit that one of my strongest memories concerns my near addiction to wine-gums. I remember these sweets more fondly as they have since been replaced by my current dependance on American candy — a legacy of my present training association with the States. I've always had a sweet tooth! 99

to be taking longer. The world's on hold. His body tenses, the muscles rigid. The circle, too, seems smaller this time and that 40-metre line, was that so far away.

He talks to himself. It is his way of concentrating. This time he needs the reassurance. This is it, he thinks, the moment I've spent ten years preparing myself for. Don't blow it now. Show them that when the pressure's greatest, you can still function properly.

That makes him feel good. It's just another challenge. Maybe the greatest he has faced but he has met the others head on and come through. He can again. He swings his arms from side to side to relax them, and spins. Technically the throw is not

a lot better than its dismal predecessors, still thrown low from closer to his hips than his shoulder but this time there is a man behind it throwing like his life depends on it. Perhaps the rest of it does.

The two-kilogram fibreglass plate with its armoured edge flies beyond the 40-metre markers. Far beyond them. It lands more than 46 metres away. He has thrown further but not at a moment like this. The throw is worth 810 points. The lead is shrunk to 34 points but it is a lead still. Thompson's invincibility is intact.

'It was the best and the worst moment of my life,' Thompson recollects now. 'For that one moment I wasn't interested in winning. Some people shy from the high pressure moments. It was what I had been looking for, a culmination of all I had trained for. Just to be faced with the situation in an Olympics … the feeling was incredible. And I'd faced it and overcome it in the thing I'm least competent in, the discus. I'd really hit the shit out of that discus.

'You've never seen a happier man than the one who came out of that circle. I couldn't believe the sensation. There's never been anything like it for me. My whole future in terms of athletic achievement, how history would judge me, my own view of myself which was most important, all of it on a single throw. I'd always believed I could handle the pressure and now I knew.

'Athletics has to be a test. If you always play safe, what does it prove? Somewhere you have to put it all on the line. If they'd been able to get all the great decathletes in history in the same competition at their peak, it wouldn't have been any more pressure on me than I'd felt at that moment. It makes me tingle thinking of it. If I'd have no-heighted in the pole vault after that, I wouldn't have cared.'

Thompson was convinced then that he had won. Nothing could be that certain in a decathlon until its tenth event was finished. There could be a banana-skin round the next corner, a fall, an injury, or a disqualification.

Concentration to the end, or else. Yet Thompson could not see any other athlete winning this gold medal.

He could lose it. He could slip on one of those banana skins but winning was out of the control of others. All they could do now was pray Thompson would blow it.

It was not over-confidence. It was a calculated measure of the opposition. He had done his homework and was in possession of the facts. He knew within a few points every rival's capability in each event, their best performances. Hingsen's he knew precisely.

Hingsen's pole vault was not as good as his own. He was a consistent 5-metre-plus vaulter. Hingsen reached as high only on his better days.

Hingsen had thrown the javelin further than him but for two years past had not thrown it as far. And then there was the 1500 metres, the tenth part of the whole and the part to which Thompson is least willing to give everything.

Hingsen could run it faster and had run it faster but could he run it faster when it counted? Thompson believed not. 'If my life depended on it, I knew I could run 20 or 25 seconds faster than I had but he couldn't. So after the discus I couldn't see how he could beat me unless I no-heighted in the pole vault and that doesn't happen often. Last time was 1979.'

Hingsen's calculations would have added up differently. He had broken the world record for the third time only two months earlier. He had prepared perfectly, often vaulting 5 metres in training. He might match Thompson there. He could throw the javelin further and in the 1500 metres he thought he could 'blow him away'. The medal was as good as his. The victory over Thompson which was eluding him was there to be had.

When he sailed over 5 metres in the warm-up for the vault and Thompson could not get off the ground his confidence must have soared as high. He needed only to do it again in the competition to put himself in the position he had dreamed of many times — level with Thompson going into the 1500 metres. What chance then would the Briton have? This was his moment.

Hingsen blew it. Twice he failed to clear the opening height of 4.50 metres and he missed all three at 4.70 metres. He had cracked under the pressure, and he threw up in the stadium tunnel where he sought sanctuary from the scene.

The explanation he offered later was that he relaxed so completely after the warm-up that he dozed while waiting his turn to vault. He awoke, he said, feeling nauseous. Thomson cannot buy it. 'Sleeping? At the greatest moment of his life? Not a prayer. There were 90,000 of us in that stadium and 89,999 could see he was taking off too close.

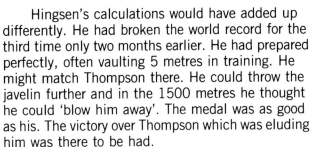

66 Apart from my favourite sweets my earliest recollection regarding the real subject of this book and my abiding passion – athletics – is that it was an area of sporting activity that suitably filled the void between soccer seasons! 99

'You should have seen the look on the faces of the other German guys. When Jurgen was attempting his third at the opening height, I caught a glimpse of them. They knew they'd move up from third to second and fourth to third if he failed. Can you imagine what they were thinking? I knew what I was, and in their position I'd have been praying he would knock the bar off.'

Thompson continued vaulting. He cleared 4.50 at the first attempt, 4.70 at the second, 4.90 at the third and finally 5 metres first time. It was worth 120 points more than Hingsen's single clearance. The lead was 152 points. Did Hingsen concede there? 'He said hardly a word to me at the Games until after the pole vault. I guess that was it for him.'

Now the question in watchers' minds was whether Thompson would break Hingsen's world record as he had broken the man. His solid first day when he scored 4633 points, 4 more than any man had scored in the first five events, set up the possibility. His javelin throw in the ninth event left him only 557 points short. (His score then of 8241 would be beaten by only four other men in the competition in ten events!) All he needed to do to own the record outright for a fourth time was run 1500 metres in 4 min 34.8 sec, 11 seconds slower than when he last broke the record two years earlier.

British newsmen, working against the tight deadlines imposed on them by Los Angeles' eight hours time difference to London, warned their offices that Thompson was on for a gold and a world record. British television viewers were advised of the possibility. It would be the only British gold that day. All attention was turned to it.

None watching would have been thinking as Thompson was.

He was 4½ minutes from achieving what he had set out to achieve nearly thirty-six hours earlier, what had occupied his mind for four years and his body for the last ten: winning a second Olympic gold medal. The world record was not important to him because it was not why he was there. 'If my life depended on it, yes,' he says now, life meaning victory. 'But when I toed the line for the 1500, it was irrelevant to what was going to happen. I did not need to break it to have what I wanted.

'I was knackered. I'd given 110 per cent in nine events. Now I was just 3½ laps from what I wanted and I didn't have to break my neck to get it. I'd done that in the other nine events. I could enjoy what was going to happen.

'Sure, if breaking 9000 points had been possible I might have had a crack. I'd say I'd needed to run 4 min 12 sec to score 9000. But it was tougher than that. So all I could get would be another world record. I'd had one of those three times and three times it'd been taken away. And the next time I get it someone will take it away from me, whether it's in a week, a month or sixteen years. It will never be mine for ever.

'Coming down the final straight of that 1500 metres it was the last thing on my mind.

'All I was thinking was two down, one to go.'

"I've always said that every man has his price!"

100 METRES

Daley's number one event. He might have been world class in it had he specialized. He has fast natural movement with rapid leg rhythm, something a man can only be born with. Coaching can increase stride length but not the number of strides a sprinter can put into a second. Indeed, scientists can tell from an examination of muscles which humans will make the best sprinters.

Reaction is another essential. The best sprinters have been shown to react to the sound of the gun in less than eight-thousand parts of a second and to have moved the first muscle in only one-hundredth of a second. In an event in which winning margins are often measured in hundred parts of a second, it can be critical.

Such speed of movement is essential to the decathlete because so many more of his events depend on it, the long jump, 400 metres, shot and hurdles. It is a prerequisite to becoming one of the best, and there is no decathlete faster than Daley.

Thompson finished in 4 min 35 sec. He missed a share of Hingsen's record by a single point, the difference in time of one-fifth of a second in one event after a competition which spanned thirty-six hours and ten different athletic events.

A year later Thompson could have been credited with that point and a half-share of the record when official re-examination of the finish photograph for his heat of the 110 metres hurdles showed him a fraction of a second faster than thought originally. It would have been the fourth time Thompson was a holder of the world record. It would have been still wholly irrelevant to his Olympics.

'If it had been my last Olympics, I'd have run faster, maybe as fast as I possibly could. Bruce Jenner did in 1976. That was great, a man who'd given everything for nine events, won his gold and still went for it in the tenth. But that was his last decathlon, the last time he would ever run 1500 metres. That's different.

'This wasn't my last. It would have been too easy to let it be the pinnacle. I needed something ahead to aim at, something to give me direction. Even if I didn't make it to 1988, it was a reason for going on until I made a decision to stop. That's why I was thinking "two down, one to go". I couldn't let Los Angeles be the end. What else would I do anyway? Work for a living? You're kidding.'

Daley with Her Royal Highness Princess Anne and Primo Nebiolo, President of the I.A.A.F.

There was a time when athletes and the clergy had much in common. There was a great deal to be said for their ways of life but nothing for the livings they offered. Only those with the most noble of motives dedicated their youth to the pursuit of such altruistic ideals. There was something else to be said for it. Nobody expected to make money from it, so none were disappointed. You came out of it with no more than you put into it and many with a whole lot less.

There were medals for the winning, and the odd tracksuit and shoes for the taking, but the prospects were not such that would persuade any right-minded parent that young Johnny was making a wise choice of career.

It has all changed now. The successful drive Porsches, buy magnificent homes and take their holidays in the Caribbean but it was the other world that young Thompson entered so determinedly little more than ten years ago.

Not surprisingly, Mrs Lydia Thompson could not be persuaded that her son was doing the right thing with his life. A part-time job at least, she argued, but no, her son knew best. An athlete could not work and train and he was an athlete.

That was not exactly how it was said. Or nobody remembers now how it was said because it was said so often in the spring and summer of 1975 and it was said probably every which way it could be. The three-bedroomed flat in Ladbroke Grove Daley and his mother shared with his younger sister was just full of the topic.

It was impossible for Daley to convince his mother that athletics was more than a hobby and there was no convincing him that it was deserving of anything less than his full attention. So one day he decided to leave.

'How my mother felt was understandable,' he accepts now. 'She didn't think athletics was a proper career for anybody, and it wasn't. I didn't think it was myself. I never said it was. I just wanted to give it a full shot. It wasn't rebellion. You don't commit yourself to something as strongly as I did just because somebody else doesn't want you to. I felt I wanted to try it and trying it meant doing it as well as I could.'

There was never an ultimatum. There was no 'get a job or get out' decree from Mrs Thompson. There just came a day when Daley knew that he could not compromise on his decision and only worse acrimony would follow. So he moved to Maida Vale to the flat of his mother's best friend Doreen Rayment, a women he regarded as an aunt.

Perhaps, his mother must have thought, it would be a passing phase. He had been keen on football. When he was thirteen and fourteen there was nothing he wanted more than to play the game professionally. He had played at every opportunity and for the team.

With Bob Mortimore

Chelsea and Fulham Football Clubs boys' teams both used him in their forward lines.

Athletics was just something which filled a few summer weeks. His headmaster had seen how good he was at the school sports and had sent him to the local club at Haywards Heath for a few races at the end of a summer term. He had finished third in both 100 and 200 metres at the first event, a Southern League, Division 3, match at Eastbourne in June 1973, as well as winning the high jump and taking fifth place in the shot. He was versatile already but it was his speed which interested the headmaster. His first 100 metre time was 11.9 sec and he was fourteen years old.

> **❝**In 1975 Bob went to ask the National decathlon coach if I could be sent on a special course and back came the reply "You've got to be kidding, that boy is a bum and he'll never amount to anything". I always like to recount that story! **❞**

Daley's interest faded with the coming of the football season. He believed he could be good at that, and there are many who see him play today in charity matches who say he could have gone a long way in the professional game. What training he did for athletics was 'messing around' between games, throwing a shot around or seeing how quickly he could start. Only slowly did its possibilities grow on him in the winter of 1973-74.

'What I liked about it was being my own boss,' he says. 'There was no relying on others. I couldn't fully accept my dependance on others in football. I mean, you can score five yourself and your team lets in six, and you're a loser.' One day, he cannot exactly remember when, sprinting became more important than football, and his commitment to it became total. He did not kick a ball for another three years.

So, perhaps, his mother was right in wondering whether it would be just another phase. Perhaps it would disappear from his life as suddenly as soccer.

It probably would have done had a man not walked into Thompson's life the year before he walked out of his mother's. His name was Bob Mortimore and he was a former basketball player and runner who had stayed around his club after his own active days were over to coach the younger members. He was not only to save Thompson for the sport but set him on course to dominate it.

They met at Crystal Palace's National Sports Centre in early August of 1974. Thompson's summer of athletics had started well: personal bests of 23 sec for the 200 and 1.80 metres for the high jump in the Sussex Championships in May and 11.2 sec twice in two 100 metres in early June. The talent was obvious but it was still raw. When he came up against those properly schooled in their events, as he did at the English Schools Championships, his natural ability took him only so far.

That day at Crystal Palace at the AAA Youth Championships was a depressing experience for Thompson. It was raining, he recalls, and his performance was as dismal: elimination in the high jump preliminaries and the 200 metres semi-finals and last in the final of the 100 metres. Not much championship material there.

Mortimore was taking a casual interest. He was a working acquaintance of Mrs Rayment, her job in Kensington bringing her into contact with his as an accountant with the borough council. She had mentioned her 'nephew' to him knowing his involvement in athletics, and when the competition ended she introduced them.

Thompson was devastated by his performances. 'I was upset, a bit down. I didn't want to know anymore. I didn't want to play this game. I was on my own which is okay when you're winning but when you're losing you need someone to tell you why. Bob asked how I'd done and said "come over Sunday and train with us".

'My aunt was there of course. She always was. But she didn't know much about it. Her interest in athletics was me. So I thought it was nice of this guy to take an interest. Anyway I didn't have anywhere else to go, so the next Sunday I went along.'

There was nothing about Mayesbrook Park, Barking, home of the Essex Beagles Athletic Club, to impress a potential young member. Their headquarters was a hut beside a track which was tolerable in summer and unusable in winter.

"I play golf but I only wish the game was a bit faster!"

Cosford AAA Junior Indoor
Championships Final, 1975

Pole vaulting at
Mayesbrook

LONG JUMP

The objective of long jumping is just that — to jump as far as you can from a wooden board. The Greeks did it by holding weights in both hands and, by swinging them, launch themselves from a standing position. Today the jump comes at the end of a short, fast run and obviously weights would be a handicap.

An Englishman, John Howard of Chester, using 3.6kg dumb-bells in each hand, leapt 8.95 metres but the only modern athlete to approach that distance was the 1968 Olympic champion Bob Beamon. He achieved 8.90 with the advantage of the 'thin air' of Mexico City where air resistence is less because of the altitude of 7,000 feet.

The usual run-up is about 40 metres and it is acceleration there that counts about 90 per cent towards success. The jump itself is a simple act, demanding good timing more than anything. Thompson, because of his speed, has always been among the best decathlon jumpers, on several occasions exceeding 8 metres.

There was better to be found closer to Thompson's home.

Mortimore's invitation was the only difference. He alone was extending a welcome. Thompson was made to feel at home. Quickly he stood out among the sprint squad. Within weeks he set a Young Athletes League record for 100 metres of 11.1 sec. He ended the season with two wins and started the next indoors with two more.

Mortimore was more than a man with a stopwatch to Thompson. 'Soon he became a real father figure,' says Daley whose father died when he was twelve. 'I used to meet him after work at Kensington Town Hall and travel to Mayesbrook with him.'

It was a journey of an hour and twenty minutes during which Bob would insist Daley did his homework for the nine 'O' levels he was studying at Hammersmith College. Often they would talk too about athletics but enough work must have been done because Daley was to pass in all those examinations.

'I've been fortunate in my friends all my life,' he says. 'It's not that they have been a great influence on me but those closest have allowed me to get on. Their advice and knowledge has always been there when I've needed it but they've never pushed it on me. I've taken what I wanted but the mistakes have been my own.'

Doreen, of course, was there whenever she was needed, supporter, chauffeur and eventually that year landlady. Bob, too. Next into his life came Dave Baptiste, a sprinter six months his junior who joined Beagles and the Mortimore squad soon after Daley, another black athlete in a club still dominated by its traditional English 'harrier' origins. They became training partners, racing rivals and firm friends.

Baptiste was a champion already. He had won the English Schools 100 metres in 1973 when Thompson was still dreaming of football, and was quicker, the fastest-ever British fifteen-year-old with a time of 10.8 sec in a year when Thompson's best was 11.1 sec. The two became inseparable, training together, rooming together on trips and running relays together for Beagles, ten of them in 1975. 'He beat me pretty often, or, at least, he tells it like that,' says Thompson. 'See, I do know what it's like to lose.'

It did not happen often. In that first full year with Beagles, Thompson competed in twenty-seven meetings, contesting thirty-four individual events, of which he won nineteen and was second in nine. Among the victories were the AAA Junior indoor 60 metres, the English Schools 200 metres and the AAA Junior 100 metres. He also finished first in the AAA Junior indoor 200 metres but was disqualified for running outside his lane, an error he could justly blame on lack of experience because he was running indoors for the first time.

It was a fair return on the investment in training that first winter with Mortimore and a remarkable sprinting season for a boy national coach Tom McNab had refused a place on a decathlon course the previous autumn. 'He told Bob I'd never be anything but a bum sprinter,' says Thompson. 'He may have been right. We'll never know now.'

Thompson yearned at the time to be the world's fastest man. He wanted to win because anything less was a wasted effort, and he was willing to give as much of himself as it took to do it. It was that commitment again, and the difference probably between Thompson and his equally talented contemporaries. Baptiste, for instance, continued to train with him and still runs with him most

IAN WELSH

High jump, Woodford

weekends but for him there were other matters beyond sprinting, like what he would live on and how he would earn it, and after three years among Britain's ten best sprinters he drifted away from it.

Thompson's determination would have ensured he went further as an individual sprinter but we can only speculate on how far. 'Would I have done 10 seconds flat? Maybe, if I had wanted it as badly as I do decathlon. Physically, I had as much talent as a guy like Allan Wells, and he didn't do badly, did he? Whether I could have worked as hard as he did on one thing I don't know but competitively I'm as good as him — and there's none better than Allan. He's the greatest this country has ever had. On any given day if I had to put all my money on Allan or Carl Lewis when they're both at their best and it was a real important title, I'd put it on Allan. He runs at his best whenever he wants to. His achievements are incredible. I can only say that I was almost as well equipped to do it as he was.'

❝ By the time I had settled in at Crawley I realised my life had been changed forever. If I'd known what kind of trial and tribulation I was to go through I would have started decathlon at junior school but all things considered I've really had the time of my life. **❞**

Mortimore was as responsible as anybody for seeing that Thompson never found out how fast he could be. He wanted to see how good he could be as a decathlete and soon was edging him in that direction. It was not without opposition from the man himself. Thompson saw anything which came between him and sprinting as an intrusion. He went along with a couple of Beagles club-mates to a weekend training session with the South of England's decathlon coach Bruce Longden 'for a bit of fun', and to try a few new events.

Some he knew. He had high jumped 1.93 metres, thrown a javelin once for the club and a boys' shot for Haywards Heath. On one occasion at Dartford College of Education in a Southern League match he had hurdled, although not against other athletes. 'The officials could find only one set of hurdles, so we all had to run the 110 metres on our own, one after another.' Thompson was the slowest in 21.1 sec.

He had also run a 400 metres but in everything but the sprints and high jump, he was a beginner who was tall enough, bulky enough and fast enough to handle anything given coaching. From the spring of 1975 the Sunday session with Longden became part of his routine.

IAN WELSH

100 metres, Mayesbrook

The decathlon is not ten separate events. It is a composite, a collection of events all testing different skills and demanding different physical attributes but which must be done in relatively quick succession and in an order which adds to their difficulty.

So on the first day a competitor starts with 100 metres, requiring pure explosive speed, and follows with a long jump which needs that speed and some agility. A man perfectly endowed for the opening two events may not be heavy enough for the shot which follows and may be too heavy for the high jump which is fourth. And what specialist shot putter or high jumper would be well equipped to run 400 metres? And all that is just on day one.

On the second day, he must hurdle 110 metres, throw a discus, pole vault, throw a javelin and finally, when two days of intense competition and effort have sapped him, run 1500 metres.

'The decathlon is a compromise,' says Thompson. 'That's one of its downsides. I would like to be really fast, a 10.1 man, but training for it would take away from other events and wouldn't be worth enough extra points in return. So you compromise on the time you spend on each event. You compromise on weight, too, because you want to be heavier for shot but not so heavy for high jump. You're not perfectly right for anything.'

Points are what governs a decathlete's life. An official scoring table directs what any single performance in each of the ten events is worth in points. So a 50 sec 400 metres, a 3.99 metre vault and a 4 min 1.3 sec 1500 metres are all judged to be worth 805 points.

The table will tell a decathlete that to improve that score in each by 100 points, he must run 400 metres in 47.95 sec, vault 4.38 metres and run 3 min 50 sec. So he will choose to practise vaulting more than running because the improvement worth 100 points will be that much easier to obtain.

66 I've always had a strong interest in music and films and I reckon listening to a tape of old hits provokes more memories than any diary or cuttings book can. Music has the power to really lift me just as an emotive scene from a favourite film can encourage me to try harder. Looking back I suppose I was a lot funkier ten years ago. Now I'm more mellow. It was easier to have fun at parties then, as now its like being head-boy at school, you really do have to set the example. I can remember my favourite records of 1975 — 'Make Me Smile' by Cockney Rebel, 'I Can't Give You Anything' by the Stylistics and 'Lady Marmalade' by La Belle, a record that my friend Dave Baptiste drove us all mad with playing it non-stop on his portable music machine up at Cosford! I went to see Jaws that year and along with most other people in the audience it really scared the life out of me. I love seeing films that frighten or surprise me and I guess we all like to jump out of our seats in horror from time to time. 99

So the best decathlete in the world cannot be the best hurdler because he cannot devote enough time to it and the best hurdler who chose to become a decathlete would soon cease to be the best hurdler.

At least the best hurdler would come to the decathlon with the necessary basic ability — speed. The skills can be learned. The speed has to be there. 'Take away all the training, I'd still be quick.'

Thompson is a 'runner-jumper-thrower', his best skills in order. Hingsen is a 'jumper-runner-thrower'. Both will work most on their weaker events because there is the greatest room for improvement, ultimately hoping that all will be as good, relatively, as each other.

Today, Thompson's weakest events are discus, hurdles and javelin. 'I have probably the greatest differences between my best and worst events of any of the top guys but the weakest are still pretty good.'

When he came into the sport, he could sprint well, jump adequately and do nothing else. He could throw the shot barely 10 metres. In his first pole vault competition, he reached only 2.44 metres and missed the landing bed, cutting and bruising himself.

It was vaulting he found took most time to learn. It was two years before he was confident with it. 'I used to go up, turn round and drop off backwards. I was terrible. It's a close run thing whether Brad McStravick (another British decathlete) or I were the worst beginners. He used to climb his pole and dive over.'

The hard part is getting off the ground. 'The bar is never a problem; running with a pole and lifting off is the problem. It's such a mental thing. I've known guys who have been doing it well for years and find they cannot get off the ground one day. And it may go on for months. It's the same as having the yips when you're putting in golf.

'Any skill can be learned. It just takes practice. One day you decide you can do it and wonder why you had so much trouble the day before.'

It was that sort of challenge about the decathlon which grew on Thompson. 'I wasn't going to make a career out of decathlon. I was doing it for a laugh. In those Sunday sessions Bruce gave me the basics but only so I wouldn't hurt myself. It wasn't serious.'

His first decathlon might have been with the national junior squad in Switzerland in May but the vaulting injury prevented it. So Mortimore and Longden took him and two other Beagles to Cwmbran, a stadium near Newport in South Wales which was the venue for the Welsh Open.

It was nearly a case of second postponement of his decathlon debut. Officials ruled that the competition was not open to any athlete under eighteen. Thompson was not quite seventeen in June 1975. Mortimore and Longden protested, and an exception was made. Thompson would be the youngest in a competition in which seniors and juniors competed together but he would not officially exist. He would be classed as a 'guest'.

After two events he led not just the juniors but everybody, and his final score of 6685 points won not only the competition but was 2000 points more than any British sixteen-year-old had ever scored. By the mutual agreement of the officials and other athletes, Thompson was given the winner's medal anyway.

'Once I'd done a decathlon, I knew this was something I could be good at. I didn't think, "I am going to be Olympic champion". Just that, "I like this". I'd won of course. If I had finished second it might have been different.

'It just clicked for me. I thought, "this I can do". It was a nice feeling. I'd always thought there would be something I could do well. Now I'd found it. I started training for it seriously almost straight away.'

The final commitment came in September. Thompson returned to Cwmbran at the end of August for the AAA Junior Championships, winning with an improved score of 7008 points which was 77 more than the senior winner managed. A third decathlon against the French at Cwmbran followed quickly in which he set a British junior record of 7100 points.

'I didn't sit down and think about it and make a decision like that. For most of 1975 I thought of myself as a sprinter. I resisted changing. I was good at what I was doing. But over that spring and summer I was doing less and less sprinting in training and more and more other things. There just came a time when I no longer thought of myself as a sprinter. I suppose I became a full-time decathlete when I moved in with Bruce at his home in Crawley that September.'

CHAPTER THREE 1976

The Olympic Games was a distant dream for Thompson in 1976 but not an immediate goal. He was a beginner, learning a new sporting language and versed only in its most basic grammar. Olympics were not part of the vocabulary yet.

The decathlon was an event for the mature athlete, and Thompson was seventeen. It was an age at which American Bob Mathias became the youngest-ever gold medallist in any athletic event but that was in 1948, the dawn of modern sport.

Decathlon in the 1970s was as specialized as other athletic disciplines. Nobody came off the college football field to become Olympic champion as Mathias had. No athlete as young as Mathias had competed since in Olympic decathlon.

The modern champions were committed specialists who had served their time. The 1968 Olympic champion Bill Twomey was 29 and the 1976 winner Bruce Jenner 26, and Longden's was a five-year plan for Thompson. His road was headed to Moscow, not Montreal, and there was nothing in the schedule that called for participation in the Games of the XXIst Olympiad in Canada that summer. There were more immediate matters. Like what was he going to live on.

It was convenient for him to live in Crawley with Bruce and his wife Sue, Britain's best pentathlete (women's decathlon equivalent), but there was a more pressing reason. A transfer from his college in Hammersmith where he had passed in nine 'O' levels to a college in Crawley would earn him a £600 grant as a student living away from home. He signed up for a two-year 'A' level course in geography and biology. The Sports Aid Foundation, a private organisation formed that winter to raise money for amateur sportsmen and women, was asked to help but its earliest funds went to those with prospects of Olympic medals the following year. Thompson was not among them or among even those expected to be selected for Britain's team.

A year later, when Longden went back with another plea for help, Thompson was rejected again. The elitist doctrine still prevailed. Thompson was not to be helped by the SAF until *after* he became Commonwealth champion.

Some things have changed in Thompson's ten years. There is more help for juniors today because athletics itself is more secure financially but there is not much new about the general attitude towards decathlon in Britain.

Decathlon was not a traditional British pursuit when Thompson came into it. No Briton had won an Olympic medal since the sport's creation for the 1912 Olympics. In 1964 Britain was not represented in it at the Games, and in 1968 its best placed competitor finished thirteenth and in 1972 fifteenth.

There were as few supporters of its cause as there were participants, and only among that tiny band was any notice taken of the happenings in the summer of 1975. The decathlon was a world of its own. Even its national championships were held independently of the AAA Championships at a different venue on other days, and usually the 'crowd' could have been delivered in the same mini-bus.

There were no sponsors of decathlon, no free clothing from manufacturers for decathletes. There were no expenses for travelling to competitions and certainly nobody offering the under-the-counter payments paid then to runners at other meetings.

> 66 Money was tight but 1976 did see a breakthrough of a kind for my material well-being. Tom McNab did me some favours at this time and one of them was to get me some free shoes from Adidas. I thought I had made it when I got the free shoes and I was the happiest little sandboy you've ever seen! I went straight down to West London Stadium to try them all out. 99

Little of that has changed in Thompson's ten years. He is still (at the end of 1985) the only Briton to have scored more than 8000 points. The AAA decathlon championships are still held at a different venue on different days and there is no sponsor. 'And I've still never been paid a penny for competing in decathlons,' he says.

This was the world he was entering that winter, a world which few Britons inhabited. He was unsure of its demands and possibilities, confident that he could do well and expecting nothing more rewarding than a lot of fun.

He got by on his grant, on Bruce and his wife's generosity as his hosts and with the continuing support of Doreen who was there whenever was necessary, sometimes the chauffeur and often the 'sponsor'. That winter she was to half-fund a 'sunshine training' trip to the South of France but usually it was less expensive, but no less vital, items like training shoes. Fortunately Daley needed little more because soon there was no time in his week to spend any more.

Longden started the five-year plan with great care. The schedule at first called for only brief sessions on weekdays. Gradually they expanded until they took in Saturdays and Sundays when he was not competing.

The talk was of nothing but athletics. There was a projector in Bruce's home on which to watch the films of training and competition he had collected in twelve years of coaching, and vast numbers of magazines and books to read. 'I learned more in one year living with Bruce than any coach could have taught me in five,' says Daley.

There were competitions all over England. He competed indoors at Cosford several times. He was second in the 200 metres at the AAA indoor championships, first in the 200 and long jump at the AAA under-20 championships and when the season moved outdoors, he long jumped for Britain in Yugoslavia, his first competition abroad. His pole vault was still an interesting sight and his legs (31 inch inside leg measurement) were too short for hurdling, but he was progressing.

The AAA decathlon championships at Cwmbran would show how well he was progressing at putting everything together. They were nominated as the year's Olympic trials but that was not pertinent to Longden's plans. 'The plan didn't include it but I was thinking of qualifying, at least half-heartedly. When we'd worked out the plan it didn't occur to us I'd progress fast enough to make Montreal a possibility, but in my own mind I knew I'd had a good winter and that, given it all went well, I could make up the 500 points.'

It was those 500 that were critical. Thompson's best score was his previous competition at Cwmbran when he scored 7100. The standard set by the International Amateur Athletic Federation was 7650. A country could send one decathlete if none achieved the standard but Britain's selectors had announced it was their minimum requirement for all selections.

That was harsh on decathletes because only two Britons had ever scored as many and they were retired from competition, but if the event was to improve the stimulus had to be there. For Thompson it was just an extra challenge. His first objective was to see any improvement equal to the effort he had put in during that first winter working to a coach's schedule. The talk in their Crawley household was more concerned with the prospects of Sue winning Olympic selection when she defended her national championship a week later.

'I went to Cwmbran to see what I could do, to find out whether I had improved. That's what we're always after in decathlon. A guy who has finished fifteenth can feel pretty pleased with himself if he's done that. It's not like an ordinary race. Fifteenth there and you're nowhere. A decathlete competes with himself against what he's done before.'

Doreen and his brother Frank went to Cwmbran, and so did Longden with another of his training group, Cliff 'Snowy' Brooks. It was a friendly, informal occasion, as decathlon competitions are. Everybody wants everybody else to succeed at their own level. Doreen and Frank mingled with officials and coaches at the track side, Doreen propped on crutches after a recent hip operation.

Thompson's improvement during the winter was obvious. His first day performances (10.8 sec 100 metres, 7.40 metres long jump, 12.79 metres shot, 1.98 metres high jump and 49.1 sec 400 metres) earned him 4092 points. All were his best performances in a decathlon. By the end of the ninth event on the second day, he was close to his best previous score in a completed decathlon.

> 66 That year a course was held at Crystal Palace to judge Olympic hopefuls and I remember that afterwards we were all paraded around an open-air market in North London. The stall-holders eagerly gave all manner of goods away to the then well known British athletes in the crowd. I wasn't judged famous enough and so got nothing. 1976 of course was the year of Punk Rock, and it has made me realise that one thing I am always untouched by is fashion. I spend most of my waking hours in track suits and although fashion trends have come and gone, my wardrobe has remained remarkably restrained! 99

Now there was a real possibility that he might beat the Olympic standard. He was 624 points short of it with the 1500 metres to run. He would need to run 4 min 24 sec, 10 seconds faster than his best. 'It seemed a long way away even then,' he admits.

Brooks walked over to say he would set the pace for the first 800 metres. He had competed in the 1972 Olympics for his native Barbados but was out of contention in these trials and was happy to sacrifice himself. 'Decathlon's like that,' says Thompson. 'You only really compete with those within a couple of hundred points of yourself.'

Mike Corden, an athlete from Sheffield, was alone in that group after nine events. He could also qualify but would have to run the 1500 metres faster even than Thompson. Everybody wanted them both to succeed. Everybody was urging them on. Tom McNab, the coach who had dismissed Thompson's sprinting prospects, appealed for more effort over the public address. Doreen screamed times from the trackside. And Brooks became so caught up in the enthusiasm that he ran the first 800 metres too fast.

'I was just trying to beat Corden, and we must have passed each other ten or eleven times. I knew I needed 4.24 but Corden was my only concern.

Bruce Jenner (U.S.A.) wins the 1500 metres in the decathlon at the 1976 Olympics, Montreal

66 Although 1976 is remembered for the Olympic games in Montreal, I had in fact been there earlier in the year to take part in an indoor international competition. I remember a moment when we were all on the team coach and someone suggested that we would all have a great time on our return for the Olympics. Of twenty confident athletes only myself and one other did in fact compete. Fortunately I live for the moment and hadn't planned too far ahead and although I made it, this incident endorses my point of view. 99

SHOT

The shot is an event almost certainly of Irish descent and it was there and in Scotland that it became most popular in the nineteenth century. The best throw of that century was by a Scot who hurled the 7.25kg ball 17 metres.

Today's decathletes do that. The specialist shot putter, a man almost certainly at least 1.88m tall and 110kg in weight, will be throwing more than 20 metres. The techniques, however, are the same, a sudden shift across the concrete circle and the hand pushing rather than throwing the shot off the shoulder.

Some throwers do use a discus-style turn which is allowed. World records have been set this way but it is an inconsistent method and never used by decathletes.

"If you wonder why I look like this I would say, Have you ever put one of these cold things under your chin?"

For me, it seemed still about winning. He had more presence of mind and was going for the time that would get him to the Olympics.' After Brooks dropped out, Panayiotis Zeniou, a London-Greek Cypriot who had won the AAA title a year earlier, took up the lead. 'He was urging us on, talking to us, telling us we should go quicker. It was crazy. Everybody was helping two guys. They were so happy for me at the end.'

Zeniou won. Thompson was second — 1 second behind him in 4 min 20.3 sec, the fastest of his life. Corden was third. Thompson's score was 7684, 34 points above the standard and almost 600 more than he scored at Cwmbran nine months earlier. It was the highest score by a seventeen-year-old of any nationality and the most scored by any decathlete in a competition in Britain.

Corden just missed the standard by 19 points — he was to achieve it later — but Thompson's place in Montreal was assured although the selectors kept him waiting nearly two months for confirmation. He would be the youngest since Mathias to compete in the decathlon, and the youngest man on Britain's athletics team.

'Qualifying would have been enough because I'd done the best I could. I didn't give much thought to the rest. It all seemed a bit far away.'

66 Montreal was my baptism of fire. It taught me to take no notice of the huge crowds and I was too young and too confident to be awe-struck. I was there for the ride and I knew I wouldn't win anything. I was there to prepare myself. I knew I was good and if I could get into the top five at the next Olympics and have a chance at a medal, I would be happy. In ten years I have been down but never out. I am irrepressible and an incurable romantic, I believe in the ultimate hero and that if you're really good you can overcome everything. I believe we have a strong hold on our lives and we have to make the ultimate decisions. Opportunities are limitless. I was equipped for the future. 99

The Games themselves he remembers as 'wonderful'. He could hardly believe it was happening to him. 'I'd read of all the famous people, seen them on television, and here I was meeting them, sitting down to dinner with them, talking to them like an old friend.'

He met Brendan Foster, the European 5000 metres champion and a world record holder, on the team plane. 'He sat down next to me and said "You're Daley Thompson, aren't you?" and I thought "yeah, that's me. He knows who I am". Apparently he had read about me in *Athletics Weekly,* and he was really pleasant.

'There was not time to be nervous at those Games. I was too busy having a good time. The competition was secondary. It was just being there to sample the atmosphere. I was training not to do anything. I was having a good time learning. You can't understand how different the atmosphere of a big Games is until you've sampled it.'

Thompson and Corden shared a room with eight others. 'It wasn't that enormous either,' he remembers but he was happy just to be there. 'Every room had a television with channels tuned to all the competition venues, so what events I couldn't get to, I watched. I was collecting every scrap of information I could use for later.

'One thing I learned was to be able to relax at the Games. Most people find that very difficult to

The opening ceremony at Montreal

❝ Apart from the Olympics I remember 1976 as a really good year for films and I particularly enjoyed *The Omen, All The President's Men, The Shootist* and *The Return of the Pink Panther*. Although all the Pink Panther movies seem to merge into one in my mind, I really think some of the individual sketches and snatches of humour are brilliant. I can remember listening to Paul Simon's 'Fifty Ways to Leave Your Lover' and enjoyed 'Shake Your Booty' by K.C. and the Sunshine Band. **❞**

do the first time which is why experiencing it when it wasn't important for me was useful. There's no real point in worrying about anything that's wrong. It's too late to do anything about it. Its time to sit back and enjoy yourself.

'I love the atmosphere of a Games, seeing the people you've read of in other sports, talking to them, just being around with other sports people. I feed off it. It's a shame so many athletes feel they want to live out of the Village these days. I think the Village is one of the best things about a Games.'

There was a third experience Thompson has not forgotten. Opening ceremonies. He walked with the British team in Montreal. When they were standing in their smart blazers and the women in lovely dresses and straw boaters, the organisers released a thousand white pigeons to symbolize peace. The poor birds, who had been locked up for three days, immediately declared war. Those standing exposed in the arena below became the target of their frustration. It was the last straw for Thompson. He has avoided all opening ceremonies since, even when offered the chance to carry the

national flag. 'Who needs to stand around for hours before his competition anyway?' he says.

In the Olympic competition his rise to the top in Britain was put into a truer perspective. He was eleventh after the first day and was eighteenth at the finish but his enjoyment of it was unrestrained. Bruce Jenner's world record which won the gold medal was so far removed from his own performance level that he was little closer to understanding its magnitude than the average spectator.

'It was out of my league at the time,' he says. 'It just seemed to me that there was nothing I had seen there that I couldn't beat one day, given enough hard work. I thought I might be in the top six by 1980, maybe among the medals, and that by 1984 I could win it.'

Four weeks later others joined in that view when he smashed the British and Commonwealth record in Talence in France with a score of 7905, a world best for any junior.

Jenner himself mentioned Thompson as his likeliest successor in a magazine article.

Thompson's plane arrived so late that he was forced to change in the taxi taking him to the arena but he scored personal bests in four of the first day's events, finishing fourth in a competition won with a European record score by Alexander Grebenyuk.

It was his first world-class performance, and it came, ironically, in a competition put on by the French in a vain attempt to launch a decathlon career for their new Olympic 110 metres hurdles champion Guy Drut. 'When I finished the 1500 metres Drut was 30 metres ahead but with a lap to go and he dropped out. Can you imagine? All that way to drop out with 300 metres or so to go! I don't think he was enjoying it.'

Thompson was. 'That was fun, lots of pbs [personal bests]. It was all fun then, I wouldn't have been doing it now.'

The marathoner who ran for five hours every day of his life, however leisurely his pace, would never finish a marathon. The damage to body and mind would be devastating. His efforts would be self-defeating.

Yet every day a decathlete determined to be the best in the world will train for five, possibly six hours, knowing that nothing less will achieve his objective. The practice and perfecting of ten events cannot be done in less. Training to run, jump and throw just takes that much longer than training to run, jump or throw. It is the millstone every decathlete must carry.

The variety of training which ten events offers lightens his load but he must like what he does to drive himself to do it so intensively for so many hours. 'It must be fun,' is Daley's dictum, 'or it is just another job and no way then could you do it day in, day out.'

For the last eleven years it has been a lot of fun for him. Not every minute of it, of course. 'Some of the time I'd prefer to be somewhere else and other times I'm going through the motions because I'm too tired or I'm injured but most of the time I get a great deal of enjoyment from it. Having the boys there helps.'

The 'boys' are the group who, sometimes singly and more often in twos and threes, have trained with Thompson throughout his years in decathlon. They have kept each other company, made each other laugh, stimulated each other and ensured that at times when one of them doesn't want to do it, there are others there to make sure he does. 'If they can go through it, it's the least I can do to turn up. You can do it alone but it wouldn't be nearly as much fun and I don't think any of us would have been able to go on so long. You have only limited enthusiasm.

Use it up and you can't replace it, and on your own it would take so much more resolve.'

The group gathered in the first three years he was training. Baptiste was the spin-off from his sprinting. Richard Slaney (later to marry Mary Decker) was a giant discus thrower he first met at the 1974 Sussex schools championships and ran into again in the college library in Crawley. 'Snowy' Brooks was another member of Longden's training group at Crystal Palace. Zeniou and Greg Richards were rival decathletes.

Thompson was the constant factor because the others came and went, and came back again, but nothing has ever wholly broken those early ties, not even others' marriages and careers. 'It's much better to have a group. Five or six hours a day is boring whatever you're doing. It's easy to get stale. When you have inter-action, things don't seem as hard. You laugh and joke and have someone there just to say "I'm knackered" to.'

Slaney lived in Crawley and attended the same college. The two would train together whenever Thompson's schedule called for throwing. The others he met at Crystal Palace on the three or four days Longden's schedule took them there, working out with them on each event's techniques, the exercising, the stretching, the weights and the running.

None of the others were ever to achieve as much as Thompson. Slaney became a British international and British record holder and competed eventually in the 1984 Olympic Games but that was the closest the others came. Brooks' greatest moment when he competed for his native Barbados in the 1972 Olympics decathlon ('he set a record for false starts', jokes Thompson) was passed when he met Thompson and he was in his early thirties already. Baptiste's

66 Back to sweets. 1977 was the year I had this thing about Topics! It was also the year I finished at college and managed to get my 'A' levels. I now rarely went to discos or parties but I do remember liking 'Tonight's The Night' by Rod Stewart, 'Car Wash' by Rose Royce and 'I Wish' by Stevie Wonder from his great album 'Songs From The Key Of Life.' 99

best came in his teens.

Even more remarkable was the persistence of Zeniou and, more recently, Richards, who was first a friend of Zeniou's and became a regular training partner of Thompson's in 1981. 'I remember way back at a squad session with Tom McNab hearing him say, "If you really progress in decathlon you could end up as good as Greg Richards" and wondering, "Who the hell is Greg Richards?". It was six years later I met him and he was a real quiet guy. All he said for a year was hello and goodbye. Now after five years together I can't shut him up.'

In ten years together neither Zeniou nor Richards scored 8000 points, a level Thompson reached in 1977, and yet they were as much help to him as he was to them. 'We are all in it to do as well as we expect to do, and we all have different levels of expectation,' says Thompson. 'We want to help each other achieve the best we can. There are days when I don't want to go to the track but then I think that they will be there, so why don't I go to help them out even if I don't do anything. And as soon as I get there they say, "Let's start" and I can't be bothered to take the harassment, so I start as well. Our goals are not the same and that's what makes it possible. We're doing the same thing but at different levels.'

It is a small circle, never more than about six, and after ten years those who are not regulars still turn up occasionally. There was never much time for socializing but what little they did they did together, spending Christmas at each other's homes

Daley, Dave Baptiste and Bob Mortimore in Luton

IAN WELSH

40

and holidaying together. Thompson, when he became well known and was invited to occasions such as film premières, would wangle invitations for others. Sometimes he would not go if this was refused. The major social event of the week was always the hour or two spent at a fast food restaurant on Saturdays after the morning session at Battersea Park.

Zeniou, who is now married to long jumper Carol Earlington and has a full-time job lecturing, is the longest-serving of the regulars. He teamed up with Thompson in June, 1976, when training took them to Crystal Palace on the same day. 'Zeni was the big man then,' says Thompson because his friend was national senior champion but since Thompson had scored more points winning the same year's junior title it must have been obvious then which of them would go further.

'Zeni is the joker. He makes us laugh. Always has. It doesn't seem like work so much when Zeni's around. And he'll always give me a straight opinion. He says what he thinks, not what he thinks I want to hear. I know I can rely on him and I can't believe he's still going. The other Saturday we did a really hard session and were all knackered and in the last run, he shot off. We all knew he was going to die halfway round but for courage and balls he takes some beating. It took us so long to pass him and because of it I did the time I should in that run. That's Zeni.'

"Zeni and I contemplating the finer points of lady mud wrestling"

HIGH JUMP

High jumping was an event limited in the early part of this century by the problem of landing. Shallow sand pits were the only protection, so most techniques were devised to enable a jumper to land on his feet. They had fancy names, like scissors, Eastern cut-off, Western roll and eventually straddle.

Since 1968 the most effective technique has been the Fosbury Flop, named after its inventor Dick Fosbury. It involves a jumper approaching the bar in a curved run and clearing the bar face up and head and shoulders first.

Fosbury won the Olympic title doing it but it became possible only because of vastly improved landing beds made of foam.

The world record has risen 11cm since his invention, and, although it looks difficult, it is the least difficult of all the techniques for the beginner to master well. The difficulty lies in achieving the necessary speed in a short run-up while keeping the consistent stride length which will bring the jumper to the same point in front of the bar each time. In any case it suits tall, light men more than decathletes.

Richards was a member of the national junior squad as far back as 1974. McNab saw great promise in him but knee injuries restricted him and between 1981 and 1984 he was unable to compete. Yet he never stopped training, and as work demanded more of Zeniou's time so his friend Richards took over as Thompson's seven-day-a-week partner. 'Knowing what he's been through, how can I complain about the work?' says Thompson.

Each helps in his own best area. Zeniou is the best 1500 metres runner and javelin thrower. Richards is best in discus and, technically, in hurdles although Thompson has a faster time. 'We always compete so I can judge how I'm doing against them. And they are a real good inspiration.'

In 1977 Zeniou was with Thompson in Madrid when he scored 8000 points for the first time. It was a match there for Britain against Spain, Denmark and Italy, in the hottest week of the Spanish capital's summer. 'Me and Big Zeni,' recalls Thompson smiling. 'That was a goodie. We had a lot of fun. Boy, it was hot, above 30°C.'

It was a stunning performance. At that time only fifty-two athletes had scored as many as 8000 points, and only fifteen had ever scored more than 8190 points which Thompson amassed. Personal bests in the 100 metres, shot, high jump and 400 metres — his time of 47.4 sec was faster than the

66By 1977 I had left Bruce's house and now shared another with two fellas, Dave Smith and Ian Prebble. We used to have a real fun time. One of the lads was a landscape gardener and the other a bouncer in a London nightclub. The bouncer got home at four in the morning and the landscape gardener had to leave for work at five-thirty in the morning. The only time all three of us were together was from five to five-thirty in the morning and I was woken up and forced to have breakfast with them at this un-godly hour so they could chat to me. I was really grumpy, I don't know how they put up with me but considering the time I don't know how I put up with them. Still we did have great fun and of course there was *Star Wars, Rocky* and *Marathon Man* on at the pictures. The film that really caught my imagination though was *Close Encounters of the Third Kind.* It really made me think. **99**

winner of the United Kingdom Championships had a month earlier — helped his first day score to 4437 which only two great decathletes, East Germany's Joachim Kirst and former Olympic champion Bill Twomey, had ever bettered. Further personal bests in the 110 metres hurdles and pole vault pushed the total score to a British and Commonwealth and world junior record.

To score 8000 points is a performance as significant to a decathlete as a sub-four minute mile was to a miler before it became commonplace. No other Briton has ever achieved it, even given the nine years since Thompson broke the duck for his country, and he was then a month short of his nineteenth birthday.

'Other people became more excited than I did,' he says. 'I was pleased because it was more than

I had scored before rather than because it was more than 8000. I could see it was a stepping stone, like 7000, but I was too young in the event to see the real significance. It wasn't the score that was important to me, only bettering the last score. I remember thinking, "I can do 8190 — next time I can do 8300".'

It was not to be, at least not on paper. Four weeks later in the European Combined Events Cup semi-final in Sittard in Holland, Thompson won but with a score of 8124. He was disappointed but he need not have been. The Madrid performance was hand-timed by officials. In Sittard automatic electronic timing which is more accurate and invariably shows slower times was in operation. Thompson's second decathlon score of the season was intrinsically his best. Zeniou, who scored a

personal best of 7204 in Madrid, improved in Sittard to 7256 and Britain qualified for the Cup final. It was a splendid weekend to celebrate Thompson's nineteenth birthday.

It was a busy year for him. He had run seven indoor meetings and a further fifteen outdoors before Sittard including winning the AAA long jump championship but it was far from finished for him. Ahead was the European Junior Championships in Donetsk in the Soviet Union and his fourth decathlon of the summer, the most he has contested in a single season.

Obviously as world junior record holder he was starting favourite. He was in great form, winning three events he contested for Beagles in a GRE Cup semi-final match two weeks earlier, and at last his pole vaulting was a viable proposition. In Madrid he had cleared 4.80 metres, in Sittard 4.70 and, just three days before he left for the Soviet Union, he vaulted 4.90 at Crystal Palace.

Yet, it was nearly a disaster. He hated the food, found the two hour time difference unsettling and the atmosphere in the Ukrainian town depressing. To make matters worse, his starting blocks slipped in the 100 metres and he stumbled, recovering only to a time of 11.02 sec. He led overnight but not by as much as he would have liked and on the second day the lead all but disappeared with uninspired hurdles and discus and a disastrous pole vault in which he cleared only 3.80 metres.

Thompson's composure deserted him. He walked away from the track to his bedroom close by. 'My world seemed as if it was falling apart,' he says. 'I was away for the best part of two hours, and came back with the clear idea of dropping out after the javelin if I had no chance of winning the gold. I didn't want to know about bronze or silver. I might as well have been last.'

There was trouble in the javelin, too, but not just for him. The Soviet officials had provided only 90 metre javelins, the type intended only for the best of specialist javelin throwers. Junior decathletes would never have been able to make them come down point first. Fortunately, one of the German team, a certain Jurgen Hingsen, had had the foresight to bring his own spear. 'Like a fool, he let everybody use it,' says Thompson. 'Really good of him. I have to say he's one of the good guys.'

Thompson's javelin throw of 49.72 metres was not his best but it was good enough to keep him in contention and persuade him it was worth continuing. He ran the 1500 metres in 4 min 35.5 sec which was well within himself, and won the gold medal by 83 points with a score of 7647. Just 123 points behind in third place was the generous owner of the only javelin, Jurgen Hingsen, a man who was to become the second best decathlete in the world .... after Thompson.

Commonwealth Games, 1978

66 I remember 1978 for the Commonwealth Games at Edmonton — a great Games and a terrific atmosphere. I will always remember 'Three Times a Lady' by the Commodores being played time and time again down in the disco. Edmonton was the most fun games I've ever been to. The Commonwealth Games doesn't have the same pressure as a major games and yet it does have the same atmosphere as a major event. People generally don't take the Commonwealth too seriously and an atmosphere of friendly competition prevails. The European Championships that same year were held in Prague and that was a contrast — heavy grey buildings and unfortunately a second place for me! 99

There was another German who figured largely in Thompson's life before Hingsen: Guido Kratschmer, bronze medallist at the European Championships of 1974 and runner-up to Jenner in the 1976 Olympics. He was Jenner's logical successor, a blond bull of a man a little taller than Thompson and a lot heavier who had set two German records in 1976 and was their national champion every year between 1975 and 1980.

The farmer's son from Grossheubach was a star in West German athletics. He was a student at the University of Mainz but not for the financial reason which had taken Thompson to Crawley. Kratschmer's needs were taken care of by the Sporthilfe, the much wealthier equivalent of and model for Britain's Sports Aid Foundation, which gave him living expenses and paid for trips to warmer climates in winter. He studied physical education and biology and, right on the campus, he trained in Mainz University Sports Club's magnificent facilities.

Thompson, in contrast, was unemployed now. He was a full-time decathlete, having passed his two 'A' levels at Crawley and decided that he could not spare any time for distractions like work and studies. There was a little money in his pocket from a toiletry company's scholarship fund and token support from the British Amateur Athletic Board ('enough to pay the milk bill'). It was not much but it was enough to persuade the SAF that he could cope without them.

The two met for the first time — not counting the 1976 Olympics where they might as well have been in different competitions — in Gotzis, a tiny place not much larger than a village near the borders of Austria where they meet Switzerland and

Liechtenstein. 'The middle of nowhere' was Thompson's first impression but for all decathletes it was often the centre of the universe, the one place where they could be certain that each year the best in the world of multi-events would gather and be welcome. Thompson was there first in 1977 when he set a British record in third place and again to meet Kratschmer a year later.

'You wouldn't believe that from such a small town so many turn up for the decathlon but there's eight to ten thousand people every year; it's like a fair, everybody happy and clapping and enjoying it, and all the best guys turn up. They appreciate what this little place does for them. It's real fun for us. I didn't go with any great expectations. I'd won the European Junior Championships but I'd no idea then how good I was. I'd been working hard towards the Commonwealth Games but I hadn't thought I was going that well that early. I didn't go to Gotzis with any thoughts of winning the European Championships later in the year.'

Why should he? There were two Soviets ahead of him at the end of 1977 in the year's ranking lists and, of course, there was also Kratschmer who had not competed in 1977 with any seriousness. So finishing second to him in Gotzis was, as he says, 'fine'. Yet how close he came to winning. After the first day he was leading by 51 points. His second day score was his best ever. From somewhere Kratschmer found more, a great second day total of 4076 points which beat Thompson by 172 points. The Briton's was again a national and Commonwealth record, 48 points more than in Madrid twelve months earlier, and 500 points more than any Commonwealth athlete had scored. He would go to Edmonton in Canada's oil province of Alberta that August with a greater margin of superiority in his event than any athlete in the Games.

Kratschmer and Thompson became friendly much later. 'It wasn't until 1980 that I realised he spoke English. Then suddenly he started talking to me.' But even before that there was a mutual, if silent admiration. 'At one competition I admired a sweater he was wearing, and when he found out it was my birthday that day, he took it off and gave it to me. Of course, it's easier for me to show my respect to him now he's not the main opposition.'

There were no 'real rivals' in Edmonton and Thompson went, complete with chief supporter Doreen, knowing that for the first time in a major games he should win. Zeniou was there, unexpectedly. England had not chosen him but Cyprus, where he was born, had. 'He never said a word to me, just came to the airport to see me off. A few days later I'm in Edmonton and this guy puts his hands round my eyes from behind. He had to persuade me he wasn't on his holidays.'

Zeniou came fifth. Thompson was in a class of his own. After five events his score was more than had ever been scored on a first day, a massive 4550 and including a long jump of 8.11 metres which only Olympic champion Lynn Davies among British jumpers had ever bettered. Only the strong wind

which aided him ruled it out as a potential record.

The second day was not as good but his final score of 8467 points was world-class. Only three men had scored more and none so young, and because it was the most outstanding athletic performance in Edmonton, the world took note and the Canadians took him to their hearts, delighting in his insistence that all competitors take part in his lap of honour and join him round the rostrum when he received his medal.

Only the British Press was less than fulsome in its praise. Thompson declined to attend the traditional winner's press conference immediately after the medal ceremony. It was late. He wanted to join Doreen for a meal. 'I'll give a press conference later,' he told officials. He did the next day but immediately epithets such as 'arrogant' and 'brash' began attaching themselves to his name. 'I was ordered to that press conference, like it was an audience with the Pope. It wasn't good enough that I would go later. They couldn't understand that I had my aunt there and wanted to see her. She deserved five minutes of my time after travelling that far. I guess that's how my trouble with the Press started. That was the first of their sniping anyway.'

With Jurgen Hingsen during the 1978 Commonwealth Games in Prague   *Inset opposite: Daley and Doreen*

400 METRES

The distance came probably from the Greek event called diaulos, which meant literally 'two lengths'. It referred to the length of the stadium at Olympia which was 192 metres. Today it is the longest of the sprints, a complete circuit of the standard track.

Few athletes can keep up an all-out sprint over the entire distance, as they can in the 100 and to some extent in the 200 metres. Fatigue sets in after three-quarters of the distance. So a runner attempts to pace himself economically, not so fast in the first half that he is tired in the second.

Traditionally, coaches ask for a fast first bend, a relaxed run down the back straight and the big effort off the last bend. That should mean the first half of the race is run not more than two seconds faster than the second.

It has not ceased to this day. Longden filtered out any unnecessary contact between Thompson and the media until 1980, and the answerphone at Doreen's home did the same job later, but what began in that misunderstanding in Edmonton soured the two side's views of each other for ever. Thompson feels the media was not interested in understanding his event, and the media could not understand why Thompson never took the opportunities to explain. Today, those he speaks to among the British Press are as small in number as his training group, and just as defensive about him.

'Popular papers are too lazy to take time to understand an event like mine, and because they don't understand they don't come. And among the heavy papers are these old school types who don't seem to like a boy like me with a mind of his own. It doesn't worry me unless they hurt my family and friends and most times they know it's not the truth. How would the media know the truth when I don't talk to them?

'Really Britain's Press only cares about people who put one foot in front of another (the runners),

Alan Drayton and Daley, August 1978

so why should I have time for them. I don't need a good press. As long as I keep winning they can't say too many bad things about me as a decathlete and what they write about the other side of me is an intrusion anyway. I still go to press conferences now because the British aren't the only ones there. I've nothing against the foreign Press. Why should I take it out on them by not going? Most of them take far more trouble understanding events like the decathlon than the British.'

So that night he went out to dinner with Doreen, and they pushed the boat out, a good restaurant and an expensive meal. Only he did not have to pay for it. The owner refused to present the bill. Thompson was a hero; he would be happy if he would be his guest. It was the first sign that his life was changing. Suddenly his time was not his own. Interviews everywhere, autographs, phone calls, offers. The demands were enormous.

It was fun. Who would complain when a London taxi driver refused to take a fare? Or offered it free in exchange for his autograph. 'I had not changed. It was people's attitudes that had changed. They expect you suddenly to be different, to be some sort

of perfect person, to have all these learned opinions on every subject. But I hadn't changed. I was still just a decathlete, having fun. I suppose I enjoyed the attention at first. I was flattered. It's only later you realise it doesn't mean anything. You're still the same guy.'

Thompson was to have no time to become accustomed to it before his next major test, the European Championships in Prague three weeks later. This was the Super League compared to the Commonwealth Games. Kratschmer would be there. So would Aleksandr Grebenyuk, world number one in 1977, and his compatriot Valeri Kachanov. So, too, would Siegfried Stark, of East Germany.

'I'd never expected that year to win the European Championships, not two months before, not even one. It only dawned on me that I could win after the Commonwealth and then I could still see Kratschmer beating me. Not the Russians, mind. They'd beaten me in Tallence in 1976 but I was a novice then, so I didn't rate Grebenyuk as a possible winner of the European.'

This time Thompson was on his own. Britain did not send a second decathlete. He was lonely,

66 Contrary to popular belief I do not have any special diet and forget to take any vitamins so they aren't much use to me. I like to eat anything that is quick to cook, and a lot of it. I hate cooking myself and the time spent cooking and preparing a meal just does not seem to be economic or efficient enough to me. It only takes a minute to eat a meal that's taken an hour to cook! Provided you have a well-balanced diet, I'm not sure there is a great need for food supplements.

Morally I think drugs are wrong. It's cheating and sport at whatever level should not be about cheating. I know why people take drugs — it's because they want to get better via a short cut. I don't condone it but I do understand and I am aware that drug-taking goes on. Athletics is just a reflection of society as a whole and until we clean up society, how can we clean up sport in general? One of the problems is that morality has to be shared between officials, doctors, and athletes. We do have to take the responsibility of putting our foot down; sport should be free for all who want it.

I take a similar view on the amateur or professional argument. The problem is people like me are professional in everything but name — dedication and application have to be 100 per cent all the time. However, the people that run the sport are amateurs , they only do it in their free time. I don't think you can organize people as specialist and as serious about their work as we are, if you only do the job part-time. The administrators should be paid. When you're in an honorary position, it is difficult to be criticized or reprimanded. The public has always had a high regard for sports people and I think they would accept that administrators should take some of the responsibilities for sport off the athletes. Most governing bodies are living in the dark ages but it would be difficult to change things as the bureaucracy is so intense. 99

and the weather was cold and depressing. It rained so often he changed four times on the first day. It was not fun, and there was pressure, the pressure of his own expectations against the most serious competition he had met.

Guido Kratschmer

In the 100 metres Kratschmer ran only a few strides before pulling up. He had arrived wearing a heavy bandage on his right thigh and had never given himself much chance of completing two days. Thompson won that heat and was winning after the first day. The second day was different. He vaulted like his old self, badly. He was far below his performance in Edmonton.

He was being casual. He did not measure his pole against the bar before jumping, and failed to realise other competitors had moved the uprights to suit their take-offs. At 4.30 metres, after he cleared the bar, the wind took his pole against the bar knocking it off. He threw his best in the javelin but Grebenyuk threw further still and took the lead for the first time.

'I think Kratschmer's dropping out made it worse for me because he was the only guy I had thought might beat me and with him gone I couldn't see myself not winning. I was that confident.' Again, as in the European Junior Championships, his composure left him. He walked away from the competition. If he could not win, he did not want to take part. When the gold has been all but your's what use is the silver?

'It was then I bumped into Brendan Foster. I can't remember where exactly but I guess he was warming up for his race. We sat and talked, and he said, "You know I've always found it's better to go home with a silver or a bronze than nothing at all". I hadn't thought about it that way. I think it persuaded me to run.'

Thompson needed to break Grebenyuk by 8.5 seconds in the 1500 metres to win the gold. He beat him by 1.6 seconds after being so badly bumped by the other Russian Kutsenko that he was forced off the track. British officials protested but the result stood. Thompson was second, a silver medallist.

'The disappointment wasn't that I had expected to win so much because before Kratschmer went, I didn't. It was because I'd blown it when the chance was there. I had lost when I should have won. I couldn't take that in. I had lost because of what I had done. That was the terrible part. I'd been in such a hurry to collect my gold, I hadn't been careful. I don't think it was over-confidence; I just lost control of myself. It was pretty depressing at the time but it wasn't a bad thing for me in the long run. If I'd won there, I might have thought it was too easy, that there was no challenge for me in the decathlon. I might have become bored with it in a couple of years. Instead I had seen what it can do to you. I was so depressed I can't believe it now. I just threw myself back into training after very little rest. I wanted to put it behind me, get it out of my system. People close to me were pretty good. They tried to understand and console, but how could they? They hadn't lost something that was theirs. I've never felt worse about anything.'

CHAPTER SIX 1979

Among the offers which poured into Doreen's new home in Worcester Park, in Surrey, were those from American universities. Some had been on the phone to him in Edmonton as soon as he won the Commonwealth title; others phoned England, or wrote. All wanted his all-round skills to bolster their college teams and they were willing to offer him financial scholarships in return. In late 1978 Thompson put together a tour of those which most interested him, his first trip to the United States.

What he saw did not attract him to the universities; it did attract him to the country. 'I went with an open mind about the offers,' he says of the tour he made of six of the twenty making offers, 'and I liked some of the places. What I didn't like was the commitment. Some of the universities said I would only have to compete once or twice a year for them but I wouldn't have liked to be part of a team and not feel part of it. I would have felt I had to compete, so I decided that it would be nice to be in the United States without being a member of anything.'

San Diego State University was the place he chose, a choice which for Richard Slaney led to an introduction to assistant track coach Joe Brinski and eventually a scholarship. The temperature never falls below 15°C in mid-winter, it rarely rains and, once Slaney was installed there later in 1979, there was a training partner on site. He was to return there twice while Slaney was there and has since stayed for up to eight months at a time in other parts of Southern California, using university facilities but renting his own accommodation.

> 66 I do like the American attitude to success. People are allowed to get on there, and are positively encouraged to be aggressive about whatever they want to do. In England there's too much of the attitude that it's not quite the done thing to be seen trying too hard, the old school thing. Our media is dominated by that.99

There was an occasion in 1982 when BBC Television viewers chose him as the Sports Personality of the Year. Nobody was told in advance of the result, and Thompson was dressed casually in the leisure wear his clothing sponsors Adidas give him. He could not see anything unusual in a soprtsman wearing sportswear to a gathering of sportsmen and women but he gave his critics a perfect opportunity for accusing him of accepting payment to dress that way when microphones picked up a four-letter expletive he used to express his surprise at the result. 'I wasn't thinking where I was

when I said it but why have a go at me for not wearing a suit and tie?

'In Britain there is this attitude we should be as people imagine us to be. I am fairly ordinary really. I just happened to be good at decathlon. Yet there is this wild idea among the media that I range from being a great guy in the arena to an arsehole in other places. I'm not. I'm like millions of other guys in how I act. I don't often wear a suit and tie and I don't often escort old ladies across the road. Why can't people accept me like that instead of imagining I should be a knight in shining armour? I find it so different in the States, so much more positive. There they judge you by how well you do, not how you hold a knife and fork.'

Longden was with Daley Thompson for part of his stay in San Diego, the beginning of their final long count-down to the 1980 Olympics, and there was not total agreement on the year's schedule. Thompson wanted to compete often but not in decathlon; Longden believed that he should compete in two decathlons. They compromised on one, the West German event in Flein in late July.

Thompson was more concerned with improving in individual events. Each year since 1976 he had kept diaries — he did until the end of 1982 — and in those he set himself targets for each year. Always they were over-ambitious.

The 110 metres hurdles is now a sprint with athletes aiming to skim the barriers but it began in very different fashion. Instead of today's L-shaped hurdles which fall away from the athlete at the slightest touch, the hurdler in the early part of this century was jumping solid and heavy sheep-hurdles. The hurdles used at the 1908 Olympics in London looked like five-bar gates and in keeping with the rural image the event always took place on grass rather than the cinder track used by other runners.

Today the race is a flat-out sprint which takes the hurdler only 20 per cent longer than the flat sprint does. The 106cm barriers spaced 9 metres apart come at a hurdler at one second intervals, and in that instant he must land, resume his stride and take off again. Rhythm is essential and clipping the barrier can upset that with disastrous results. Tall men dominate but it is length of leg that it is critical. Daley's 31inch inside leg measurement is a severe handicap to him.

> **❝** Each year I'd set a target for each event and in six years I only achieved three or four. Only in my decathlon score did I usually get close and then only because I thought what I should score and then took 200 or 300 points off. **❞**

Some of his individual competitions were multi-events in themselves. In the opening British League Division match of the season he competed in seven individual events, and a relay, winning in all but the javelin and discus with the javelin throw a personal best, his first of more than 60 metres. His speed was also improving. In the AAA Championships he ran 10.49 sec into a headwind for fourth place in the final.

So he went to Flein in good spirits, expecting to do well. He did, in as much as was possible, but the airline lost his poles. They returned them eventually with stickers of places as far away as Rio on them but that weekend he competed without them.

> **❝** Poles are something very personal. You can't just pick up any pole and vault with it straightaway. **❞**

He stunned the Germans on the first day, running a superb 100 metres in a best of 10.45 sec and a best 400 metres of 47.30 sec for a first-day total of 4507. It was close to his first-day score at the Commonwealth Games and was followed on day two by a scorching 14.39 sec hurdles, another best. After seven events he was up on his score in Edmonton by 44 points. Then came the pole vault. Thompson could not clear a height. So he threw the javelin a personal best of 61.92 metres and withdrew from the competition. In eight completed events his score was 6954. By even the most conservative estimates he would have scored around 8400 and more likely closer to 8500. The best score anywhere in 1979 was 8484 by Kratschmer. It was obvious to everybody that the two men would be the pair duelling over the Olympic gold medal in Moscow a year later.

It was obvious certainly to Thompson. He was leaving nothing to chance. He was busy competing — eight meetings that August alone — and training but between time there was always his 'homework' to be done, reading magazines, checking competitors' performances, remembering them.

"Before the L.A. Games I got very homesick — so I used to write home every spare mo' — honest!"

> **❝** It's vital to know what others can do. You can't afford to wait until the end of the day to find out how well rivals are doing; you have to know as it happens. You need it to psyche yourself. If they are doing badly, obviously you tell yourself you can win. If they are doing well, you tell yourself you have to do better. I know the top fifty guys' personal bests within 20 to 50 points. I enjoy the research. I split up their scores, analyse where their strengths and weaknesses are, see what group type they fall into. You don't leave things like that to chance. **❞**

66 1980 of course was the year of the Moscow Olympics and my first Olympic gold medal. It was also the year of the disastrous American boycott. It amazes me that what is arguably the world's greatest democracy can give a dictatorial command and stop people from doing something, especially as people have put four years of sweat into their preparation. It also strikes me that it is the job of the Olympic Committees to take teams to the Olympics and to give up without a fight suggests they are not performing the jobs for which they were appointed. At the end of the day it made no difference to the Russian position in Afghanistan and ruined the chances of many athletes of ever competing in an Olympics. As point of fact, because some of the African nations missed out in 1976 and 1980, they have lost a whole generation of potential athletic champions. I enjoyed 1980 but it was a sad year for a lot of people. I'm only grateful that we had Dennis Follows leading our committee and he stood firm and allowed us to do our job and compete. 99

There comes a moment before every major Games when Thompson knows he is going to win. 'Maybe it is three weeks before or only two days, whenever. From that moment I know without a shadow of doubt. Before the 1982 European Championships it happened one day when I was lying in my bath. It happened for the first time before Moscow. I went there knowing I was going to win. There was no other feeling, never any doubt, never a millisecond of doubt.'

Any doubt would have disappeared the moment he knew that Kratschmer would not be there to meet him, or any of the West Germans and Americans. On New Year's Day, 1980, a coup toppled the Marxist government of Hafizullah Amin in Afghanistan and thousands of Soviet troops poured into the country. Four days later the United States President Jimmy Carter announced his response in a speech which promised that 'the participation of athletes and the travel to Moscow by spectators who would normally wish to attend the Olympic Games' would be endangered unless the Soviet Union withdrew its troops. When his deadline of February 20 passed without it happening, the boycott by

America became official. West Germany joined it; the British Olympic Association, in spite of Prime Minister Margaret Thatcher's urging, refused.

The effect on Thompson was minimal. He continued with his planned programme, the dates of July 25 and 26 inscribed in his mind. 'Athletes are not bothered about where their rivals come from or whether they read *Das Kapital* in bed at night,' he told the Sunday Times' Athletics correspondent Cliff Temple. It is an opinion that, in hindsight, he has not changed by a dot or comma. 'Everybody knows the dates and the Olympic champion is the best there at that time. It's no good being 8,000 miles away and saying, "I would have won if I'd been there". Nobody remembers who wasn't there; only who won. He's the champion and that's all history will be concerned about. Anyway, what difference did the boycott make. Did the troops leave? Sport was just being used.'

Thompson was concerned more with events in his own life. His relationship with Longden was reaching its end. It was the only time in his ten years or more of training for decathlon that he remembers not enjoying what he was doing. 'It became a bit rough,' he says. 'There was no fun in it. For two months I was never pleased with anything I was doing. I was getting really intense. It was just Bruce and I, and I needed somebody else to bounce things off.'

Longden and Thompson had been as close as it was possible to each other for more than five years. For a year they had lived under the same roof, and they saw each other almost daily at other times,

master and student. 'We were getting very introspective. We'd learned a lot of stuff together. He knew everything about me but I knew everything he was going to teach me, and I needed fresh ideas. We were at the point where we had to make a break or stagnate.'

Longden was always the technician, the solid, knowledgeable expert. Thompson's needs now were different. 'Bruce was a good coach but he was never a motivator. He couldn't inspire me. Not that I needed it really but it would have been nice in a while. He did fine by me, helped me a lot. He was there when I needed him most in the early days. Now I needed something else.'

There was no traumatic parting, simply a drifting apart. 'I just started training with the boys more, and I really enjoyed that. It was probably what I wanted to do all along. When I was with Bruce I was there when they were but not in there with them. I was Bruce's man. I had to go off and do what he said. The boys resented it. I wasn't my own man.'

The mood hung over Thompson in the late spring. However much he drove himself in training, he arrived home dissatisfied. Nothing was ever good enough. He went to Gotzis again in May feeling that way.

66 By 1980 I realised that all my efforts and beliefs had been fulfilled and returned home from Moscow satisfied that I had done a good job. After a major competition, I start to come down from the high of winning after the first five minutes, but a week or so later I'm still really happy. My satisfaction is a very private thing and I don't like to share it with a lot of people. I miss the competition but I realise, of course, that I can't do it every week. I always like to know I'm in with a chance of doing better than before. Still, I'd love to do a decathlon a week! 99

Quite why in that frame of mind he broke Jenner's fine 1976 world record is beyond understanding. Physically, Thompson was ill-equipped for it on that sunny weekend, and yet the record crept up on him until in the end he had to have a try for it. 'The majors are all that matter; the other competitions are just to see how I'm going on the way,' he explains. 'A world record was what I wanted in Moscow. That was the place for it. Not Gotzis.'

Indeed his first day score of 4486 was down on Edmonton and the aborted competition in Flein.

Hoyte, Zeniou, Thompson, Roddan and Clark. Front row: Bruce and Sue Longden and Frank Attorn

It was on the second day that the record grew into a possibility when he achieved personal bests in the hurdles, pole vault and javelin.

There were only three British journalists there to record it, two switched there after covering a major boxing title fight in Munich. None had covered a decathlon competition before, and Longden with his little blue book of decathlon scoring tables was there source of information. Yet slowly the excitement built until I remember us conferring on the wisdom of using the one telephone in the changing rooms to alert our offices in Fleet Street of a possible world record, or keeping quiet until it was certain. We phoned London, and that only made the tension worse because now they, too, were expecting something.

Thompson, Longden was confident, would have no trouble running 4 min 26.1 sec for 1500 metres which was all he needed for the record, and British reporters raised on British passion for running and fresh from Sebastian Coe's three world records the previous summer could not believe a time so slow would be beyond him.

We were not alone. Mauricio Bardales, an American much smaller and better suited to running, was pacing him but without much interest from Thompson. 'I kept shouting at him to make his move but his body was not responding,' Bardales explained. 'But that man is all heart. Finally I kicked him into action.' Thompson's lumbering gait raised itself into something resembling the sprint of a tired man, and he crossed the line in 4 min 25.49 sec. Thompson's score was 8622 points, 5 more than Jenner.

It took nearly as long as the race to confirm the record. Longden's stopwatch put him inside the time necessary but finding an Austrian who spoke enough English to confirm it was impossible. Only their excitement convinced us. Thompson seemed the only man unaffected, and it was an impression which lasted to the evening when, without complaint and with apparent relief, he left the traditional post-meeting party at the local hotel to give the British interviews.

When he arrived home, there was a cable from Jenner: 'Congratulations. Ever since the day I met you in Montreal, I knew you had the right attitude to be the best in the world. I know you'll wear the crown well. My Wheaties contract is up in a year — I'll give them your name. 9000 or bust. Former world record holder, Bruce Jenner.'

Curiously, Thompson's dark mood was not lifted. 'Gotzis made things worse. I just became more intense, wanting to do better and better. Straight away I started training again, harder than ever. I should have left it a while but I couldn't see it.' He trained more than the schedule demanded, seeking extra sessions back with his old friends at Beagles.

Not until later did he realise how much Gotzis had taken from him. It probably inflicted such grievous harm on his condition that it cost him the world record when he wanted it most in Moscow.

Thompson's record lasted only twenty seven days. In Bernhausen, West Germany, in mid-June, Kratschmer scored 8649 points, 27 more points. Thompson sent him a congratulatory cable. He says he was not overly disappointed. Improvement in the decathlon seemed the natural way of things. 'Records don't last because they encourage others to do better. Okay, if you broke a record by 200 or 300 points in one go you'd kill it for a few years, like Beamon did in the long jump. But I'd gone 5 points better than Jenner; that just gave Kratschmer the incentive.'

Indeed, the breaking of his record may have been the stimulus which brought him out of his depression because in the next three weeks before he left for Moscow he competed in seven meetings and twenty-four different events. In one weekend he ran twice at Crystal Palace on Saturday and in five events at Edinburgh 400 miles away on the Sunday.

When he arrived in Moscow he was ready. He spent the last few days, just passing time, a few sprints, a bit of stretching, throwing the shot around, just letting his body gather itself for the two days of intense physical effort that was ahead.

The decathlon, as always, began early, at ten in the morning. The night before Thompson was in bed by eight and wide awake fifty-five minutes before his alarm was scheduled to go off at five o'clock. His kit-bag was packed but he checked it again to be sure: eight pairs of shoes, 'some for the different events, some just-in-case-gear ... like just in case it rains, or the sun shines or someone steals them', four sets of clothing, a load of food, sprays, tape for markers, poles, blisters and fingers, and anything else he could think of because 'it's better to have it than not have it'. Some competitors pack teddy bears or good-luck charms, but Thompson carries his own luck.

'I remember revising the night before my 'A'-level biology exam and the book fell open at a passage on sewerage. Next day, the first question: sewerage. I'm just lucky that way. If I fell face first in the sewerage I'd come out okay.'

Thompson breakfasted lightly at six, 'stole' the food and drink he would need during the day and was back in his room before 6.30. The Lenin Stadium was on another side of Moscow to the

> 66 Although the media had taken some notice of me by 1978, the Moscow Games unleashed a flood of Press and T.V. attention. I'm often asked my opinion of the media and my honest answer is that I really take very little notice of their opinion of me. By 1980 I had started to try to withdraw from any spotlight as basically I am a very private and shy guy. However, it should be remembered that in the early days of my career people in the media shied away from decathlon mainly because they didn't really understand the competition and were not prepared to learn. Really before I came along there was an enormous lack of interest in the event and even to this day people ask me about my rifle shooting! 99

Village, so transport left in plenty of time. By eight he was warming-up, a bit of stretching, a few short sprints, the same routine he had done every day for five years. Then into the reporting room, single file with the other nineteen athletes.

'If there's any time at any major championships I would like to do without, this is it, from walking from the warm-up track to the reporting room until you are on the track itself. If there is a time when I'm tense that's it. I am prepared, I am loose, I want to go. I don't need any more waiting time.'

The athletes sit on benches or jog between them. Some sprint abruptly and frantically on the spot. 'People talk but you find those talking with one another are not those who will be in competition together.' There were enough, more than enough of those for Thompson, the East Germans Siegfried Stark and Rainer Pottel, the Soviets Valeri Kachanov and Yuri Kutsenko. The others were in a different league, like the nineteen-year-old Peruvian Miro Ronac and the Sierra Leonian Columba Blango who had never completed a decathlon.

The day was dry but cool. There was a breeze whisking result sheets and plastic cups about in the press seats. On the track it swirled this way and that. In the 100 metres it was behind Thompson, helping him to a hugely superior time of 10.62 sec. In the long jump it blew into his face but he jumped an impressive 8 metres. Already the coolness was taking its toll. Stark pulled a hamstring and withdrew. Pottel could not get his run-up right and ran through three times. He withdrew after one more event. At the end of the day Thompson led by 264 from Kutsenko and was ahead of the halfway score of his world record.

DISCUS

Discus is one of the oldest athletic events. The word itself is Greek, meaning literally 'thing for throwing'. Yet in the Games of Ancient Greece it was not an event in itself but part of a multi-event called pentathlon. Just as it is in the modern decathlon.

Nobody knows precisely how the Greeks threw their discoi but when the Olympics were revived in modern times in Athens in 1896, the rules insisted that a throw should be made from a standing position on a rectangular pedestal resembling a baseball pitcher's mound. Only at the 1908 Olympics in London was a parallel competition held called 'freestyle'.

Freestyle, in which a thrower could use any method as long as he stayed within a small round circle, became the only method recognized in 1913 when the official world record was 47.58 metres. Throwers then made a half turn from a side-on starting position but now the thrower starts at 270deg to the direction of his throw, pivots through 1¾ turns before launching the discus with a straight arm throw. The best throw around 70 metres; the best decathletes around 50 metres.

The second day was colder still and it was raining when Thompson hurdled. 'I thought to myself, "One of the favourites in 1972 fell over. Jeff Bannister, an American guy. In 1976 one of the favourites fell, Fred Dixon. No way I'm going to fall". I talk to myself regularly. Easiest way to get myself to do what I want. I pretend I'm outside looking in. So I tell this guy to be calm and I'm calm. Then I say to him, "You've done this 40,000 times over the last few years, what's so difficult about it?". In the hurdles I talk myself over every hurdle. Of course, most of it comes automatically but everybody has weak points, perhaps the rear leg or landing on your toes. So I tell myself "faster, faster". You need something to concentrate on, even if it's the hurdles themselves.' He ran 14.47 sec, which was not good but it was too cool and wet for explosive hurdling. After the discus he led by 198 points and the pole vault settled it. Kachanov, who was closest to him, pulled a thigh muscle in a warm-up jump and withdrew.

It was late when the 1500 metres started, and dark. Thompson took his turn like a lap of honour. He jogged home last barely inside 4 min 49 sec. He could have broken the world record by running 4.17 but Gotzis had taken too much from him for one year. Kratschmer, sitting watching as a guest of a West German magazine, at least kept his record.

Thompson paid little attention to the formalities during the medal presentation, conducting the British group of spectators through the National Anthem and waving to his friends like Doreen and Snowy Brooks among them. He was savouring the moment. 'Usually I'm just glad it's finished, and the more I do the more I'm glad. I can't wait sometimes. I look forward to the competition but when I'm halfway through it I want it over. I don't realise until I'm in it how much I expect of myself. I have such high expectations that it takes it out of me.'

It was past ten in the evening now but Thompson's day in the stadium was not over. He was taken under escort like all winners to the dope control room where he was asked to produce a specimen of urine, the traditional method of testing to ensure athletes have not taken illegal drugs during their preparations. It is a task that usually takes seconds. Thompson was in that small room making the impossible demand on his body until two the following morning. 'The trouble was I'd been to the toilet after the pole vault and because of dehydration and lack of drink the biggest problem I had over the two days was the little 'p' afterwards.' Everywhere he went in the deserted, stone-floored halls of the giant stadium officials followed, never letting him out of their sight. When he emerged finally, everybody else was long gone. 'I'm not a great one for celebrating but one night that I might have felt like it, everybody's gone to bed.' So he wandered on his own through the Village to his single room, and went to bed himself.

'I can celebrate for the rest of my life. Right then after a competition, I'm too tired to bother. Two days later I feel real good about it but by then I have it in perspective. I know it's not the greatest thing that's ever going to happen to me. If it were, you'd never be able to pick yourself up and do it all over again next year. I try not to get too high, I enjoy it but on the inside.'

He enjoyed it all right after Moscow. He remembers the feeling. 'People must have thought me strange because I was walking round all the time with this silly grin on my face. I couldn't help it. Every time I thought of the Olympics, I couldn't help smiling.'

66 Having achieved my first gold medal, my sights were set for another in 1984 at Los Angeles and success depended on continual training and appraisal in the intermediate years. However, it wasn't all hard work. I still had fun and enjoyed the other things in my life. Music was there as ever and I can pick out 'Gino' by Dexy's Midnight Runners and 'Use It Up and Wear It Out' by Odyssey as my favourites. *Being There* starring Peter Sellers was one of my favourite films of the time. 99

It was at about this time that Daley Thompson moved from the sports pages of tabloid newspapers to sections further forward, to gossip columns, television pages and hard news. There was no greater understanding of what he did but there was general recognition that he did it better than anyone else. He was a star, young, good-looking and successful. A celebrity. He hosted a television show for teenagers. He was advising magazine readers on diet, on exercise and good living. His name was used everywhere. He was in danger of becoming public property, and he pulled back from it only just in time.

'It's nice to be in the limelight but as you get older you realise it's not so important,' he said at the time, an opinion which has hardened into a way of life over the last five years. Today, Thompson courts the public stage with the enthusiasm of a recluse, sheltering behind the protection of business associates and advisers and the well-trained discretion of his close circle of friends.

The same man who turned somersaults of joy in a most public expression of his happiness when he cleared a pole vault bar in the Los Angeles Olympics will go to extraordinary lengths to guard his privacy elsewhere and, far more resolutely, to protect his precious time. He cannot accept that anybody has a God-given right to that. It is not so much that it is an intrusion as an interpretation. He feels that time spent making himself a better athlete is more wisely spent than on anything else. Some don't agree with him. An executive for the Terry Wogan Show on BBC television, frustrated that his incessant invitations to Thompson to appear met the same answer, warned his agent: 'Just let him try to get on our show when he's on the way down.' He could not accept that Thompson felt that there were other things more important to him.

'There's so much to do of what I must that to find time for anything else means it must be really important. I don't consider very many things that important. Very, very few. Certainly not the Wogan show. I just don't enjoy being at the centre of things. I would really rather not be there.

'I just see every hour spent on TV or radio as an hour or less at the track, and I feel much more comfortable in the surroundings of a track than anywhere else, apart from home. If I have an hour to spare, I'll go to the track an hour early even just to sit and watch, or I'll lie on the pole vault bed or even just sit beside the track in my car. Strange that, isn't it? I enjoy the sport but it's sort of an end in itself. It's good enough. I don't want more. I don't want what other people think has to go with the sport.

'I'm a lucky guy because I'm doing what I do. There is nothing I would rather be doing, no people I would rather be with and no place I'd rather be

66 In 1981, I went to see another favourite movie — *Arthur*. During the movie there was a fellah behind me who kept on speaking Dudley Moore's lines. I turned round to tell him to shut-up and I couldn't believe my eyes when I realised he was wearing top-hat, tails and carrying a cane. I thought what a berk and asked him again to shut-up. During the interval, however, he apologised and told me this was the forty-sixth time he'd seen the movie! I thought *I* liked the cinema! **99**

at. And no matter how much you are paid, you can't buy that sort of happiness. But why should I pay a price for it?

'I'm not always on duty. I am a decathlete, a personality if you like, only some of the time. Most of it I am just an ordinary bloke who wants to be treated as others are, and I think I'm the best judge of when that is. You might think me strange but I don't enjoy people looking at me or staring at me except for those two days when I'm doing my thing, when I'm on my stage.'

Autograph hunters are a constant source of anguish for Thompson. Not that he disapproves. When he remembers he carries photograph cards of himself to give them. He dispensed nearly two hundred one afternoon at Cosford early in 1986 only to find himself criticized for refusing to sign his name for one young girl. 'I think I've been great with autograph hunters over the years. If I refuse it's usually because I'm in the middle of something. People do come up on impulse. They don't ask themselves, "Is he in the middle of warm-up or stretching or even preparing himself mentally?" They don't think, "If he is watching something, that's important to him". If I've been competing and showered and changed, I'm happy to sit down and sign for half-an-hour. That's okay. My thing's over. But before it or in the middle, it's selfish of people to ask.

'Okay, so I understand that I owe it to the sport to do some of these things. I just don't think I owe it to the sport to do it twenty-four hours a day. Yes, I want to be successful as a decathlete but, no, I am not interested in all the trappings of being successful at it. What it comes down to is that as long as I'm doing decathlon, I'm going to give it all the time it needs. All the time.'

66 1981 was also the year of *Chariots of Fire*, a really wonderful film which I can really identify with. I actually knew Harold Abrahams when he was Chairman of the AAA. I could understand exactly what the two fellows were doing and I enjoyed the film so much I've seen it nine times. Another series of films which captured the mood of competition for me are the *Rocky* films and the soundtrack from *Rocky II*, 'The Eye Of The Tiger', which really inspires me. In fact before the 1983 World Championships in Helsinki, I must have watched *Rocky II* eight times on the video player in our team common rooms. I also really enjoyed *Superman* and curiously it proved immensely popular with the Cuban athletes. **99**

It never stops. One training year ends on a Friday. The next begins on the Monday. Only the occasional holiday intervenes but on that Thompson is active, snorkelling, playing tennis, golf, beach games. 'I'm thinking of doing the Open University now because so much of my stuff is physical. I need something to keep the mind going.'

Daley with BBC's Ron Pickering

Keeping the training sufficiently stimulating to avoid staleness is all part of the programme. Take his general fitness work. It is always scheduled for great bursts of activity, brought to the boil for a while and then pushed onto a back burner while another aspect has its turn. The build-up is gradual but inexorable, starting low and cutting off with the crescendo.

So on day one Thompson, Richards and Zeniou will do twenty sit-ups, pull-ups, squats, squat thrusts, and press-ups. They will go through that series three or four times, and later in the day come back to do it all again. On day two, they will do it all twice but this time each exercise will be done twenty-five times. And on day three it will be thirty times until by the last day of the month they do eight sets of the exercises a hundred times each and twice in the day. 'It's probably the most boring thing we do, so at the end of the month we stop. And for the next ten or twelve weeks we only do general fitness work once a week.'

Taking its place in the programme will be a variation on the theme Thompson calls 'one minute on-30 seconds off' in which the three of them race. They will do a minute of press-ups for 30 seconds rest, a minute of squats for 30 seconds rest, a minute of sit-ups and so on. 'Zeni is really good at squat thrusts and squats. I am best at sit-ups; Greg's best at press-ups. I rarely win. In all our training we are well balanced. When we do drills for pole vault with ropes and on high bars, the others do it much better because I never did gymnastics at school — well, that's my excuse, I'm really just no good. We all have our strengths and weaknesses which is what makes it fun.'

Each day is structured to take so much work. Usually it takes about six hours of which 45 minutes will be resting. No one event is allowed to take more than about 20 minutes in one session because they find they cannot concentrate longer. But over a whole day they will have practised most of the ten events. 'We take it leisurely but we have to get through the schedule. I've woken up in the middle of the night and realised I haven't done something.'

On Monday, Wednesday and Friday mornings the others do weight training which Thompson never joins. He suffered one of his few serious injuries attempting it in the winter of 1984-85 for the first time, cracking two vertebrae when he was doing a clean lift. 'Nothing goes wrong when you do it right but I did one too many when I was tired. It took nine weeks to get over it and I've never again picked up a weight. I'd thought there's three ways to get better — get faster, improve technically and get stronger. Well, my speed's fine, my technique's getting better, so I played my trump card of strength and broke my back. I do pull-ups and chins now instead. They're safer.'

Thompson arrives at about one, warms up and does bounding until 2.45. He rests for 30 minutes and then runs, high jumps and long jumps and throws shot and discus. He will finish about 8.30. On Tuesdays and Thursdays, the difference is the running he does between eight and ten in the morning. 'And I'll start the afternoon later and not finish until 9.30.'

Somewhere he finds time to eat. 'Maybe it's on the way home. We'll stop at a McDonald's. Sometimes I cook at home. I don't live to eat, I eat to live. I do it when I want it. I eat a lot when I'm hungry. When I'm not, I don't eat. It's not an important thing with me.'

> 66 It's important to try to relax and after Moscow I did not compete for a year although I still trained vigorously. I sometimes go to concerts and at about this time saw a favourite group, Cool and the Gang in San Diego. After numerous support acts and six hours later at one o'clock in the morning, the band finally came on! I was so tired! Zeni actually managed to fall asleep through a whole Dr. Hook concert and when woken up by us all leaving exclaimed in his own inimitable way, "But they've only been on for ten minutes". He had been on a two and a half day outward bound course and hadn't slept so I guess he can be excused! 99

His diet defies the expert opinion on balanced eating. A nutritionist in Canada, a former athlete, told him he was damaging his body. For a time Thompson changed. He ate more balanced meals, better prepared. There were more salads ('which I hate'), chicken, fish and fewer potatoes. 'I was healthier but I wasn't enjoying it. So I changed back to my old ways.'

Now the staple food is chips ('you can't beat a good chip') with fried fish or burgers washed down with fizzy lemonade. 'Sometimes when I get injured I wonder whether it's my body getting revenge. I've never pampered it. I treat it more like a carthorse than a racehorse.'

He did not have Longden to keep an eye on any of his bad habits in 1981 but there was another coach in his life, a Pole Andrzej Krzesinski. He had guided two of his compatriots, Tadeusz Slusarski and Wladyslaw Kozakiewicz, to Olympic gold medals in pole vault, and was now seeking greater rewards abroad. Haringey, where he worked for the borough

Scuba diving in the Cayman Islands

council at their New Rivers Sports Centre, was his first stopping place. Soon it became the haunt of Thompson, Richards and Zeniou, as much for Andrzej's assistance as the centre's excellent facilities.

'He was so positive. He wasn't the world's greatest all-round coach but he knew about long jump, hurdles and pole vault and was enthusiastic about everything. He would inspire you to do better and after years of having to inspire myself, it was like starting again.'

Krzesinski was also experienced working with decathletes and created progressive training programmes for Thompson and the others which they still use today. Drills mostly, for jumping, hurdling

and vaulting, work with medicine balls, each calculated to ready every sinew for the demands of each technique.

Technique was where Thompson could score most extra points at that stage of his career. Always he would work on his weakest event. His 100 and 400 metres and long jump have stood still largely because it was more important to devote himself to events in which he would gain the greatest return in increased scores. So he would do eight or nine sessions a week with shot, discus and javelin but far fewer for long jumps. 'I am not a great throws technician but for a little guy I am not bad,' he says.

Repetition is the key. Sometimes he has used

POLE VAULT

It began as the 'high jump with pole'. There was even a rural sport of leaping ditches with poles. The poles were at first ash, later bamboo and finally in the 1950s light steel. It was the advent of a fibreglass pole in the early 1960s which gave the event a new dimension. In the last twenty years the world record has soared more than a metre.

The vaulter sprints down a runway carrying the pole ahead of him before 'planting' its tip in a box set into the ground. This bends the pole and drives it upwards and as it straightens the vaulter comes into a position in which he appears vertical upside down. He goes over the bar feet first turning as he does so as he faces downwards.

The movements are difficult and demand years of practice, both with a pole and in a gymnasium. Few decathletes master it completely because of the other demands on their time but Daley is regularly over 5 metres in competition.

videos to show him where he is wrong but more often Greg or Zeni's eyes. 'We are mirrors for each other.' Always they are seeking to become so perfect in technique that it comes automatically. 'The more confident you feel, the more time you have. At first everything is over in a flash. When you are more confident, you are more relaxed and then you have time to think what you are doing and not rush it.'

They worked with Krzesinski for two winters. He was being paid partly by the British Amateur Athletics Board for coaching clinics he gave around Britain but when an offer came for him to move to America's West Coast, there was a lot of back-stabbing and he lost the support here of officials who might have seen to it that he was better used. It was a real shame. He was at least as knowledgeable as any coach we had but there was lots of jealousies. We lost a good man when he went.'

Thompson was having his own problems with the athletics Establishment at this time. They wanted him to compete in the European Combined Events Cup which they had won the right to stage at the new Alexander Stadium in Birmingham's Perry Barr suburb in August 1981. Having the Olympic champion in Britain's team was an obvious plus, not least in selling the event to potential sponsors.

Unfortunately, Thompson was not going to be there. He was resolved not to compete because the British Sports Aid Foundation, in association with the BAAB, was insisting that he should compete. It was a matter of principle for Thompson. 'It was likely, very likely that I would have competed in Birmingham. Greg was likely to be competing. So was Zeni. So were most of the boys from Europe. It was the sort of place I wanted to be but I was reacting against someone telling me I had to. It's me who spends every day doing the training and nobody else is any judge of when and where I should compete.'

The disagreement was polite and private, conducted through an exchange of letters. The Sports Aid Foundation, which had paid £4,000 to Thompson in grants during 1980, asked for his year's intentions as they do all competitors requiring grants. Thompson replied that he wanted to recapture the world record. He believed that there were three possible occasions to do it — the Gotzis meeting, a match between Canada and Britain in Saskatoon and the European Cup in Birmingham.

The SAF's policy that year was to help only those preparing for 'world, European or equivalent events'. They regarded Birmingham as the only decathlon competition which fell into that category. They responded by asking Thompson whether he could guarantee his presence in Birmingham but he wouldn't. 'I can never guarantee competing anywhere,' he wrote, since it depended always on his physical condition at the time.

So Thompson received nothing from the SAF and the BAAB, who were privy to the correspondence, must have assumed that he would not compete in Birmingham.

Instead they chose to assume that he had said only that he could not guarantee it. Four weeks before Birmingham he was asked again directly by the BAAB. 'I told them we'd already settled it, and there was never any chance I would change my mind. I may have wanted to compete but no way would I have done. Nothing on earth would have made me. To have said that unless I compete at a certain event they would take my money away .... they could keep it. There was a principle involved. I would cut my nose off to spite my face rather than back down. If it was worth standing up for in the first place, it was worth standing up for all the way.'

So the story leaked from the BAAB that Thompson was in danger of losing his grant. Of course he did not have one to lose by then but the BAAB could hardly admit to that without admitting that Thompson's decision had been known for nine months. They also failed to admit that three months earlier they had also refused him permission to compete in Gotzis as a punishment for declining Birmingham, an admission which would have revealed their prior knowledge.

Thompson was presented as unpatriotic and selfish, a man who would not do his bit for team and country and took money to which he was not entitled. None of it was true and could have been shown to be untrue but Thompson was not about to defend himself publicly. 'If it's what they want to think, nothing I say will change their mind,' he says. It is his attitude to all criticism. 'As long as it doesn't hurt family and friends, I can live with it.' He has never asked for a penny from the SAF again. 'The issue was not about patriotism. It was about principle.'

He did contest a decathlon that year but did not complete it. It was in Saskatoon with the rest of Britain's senior and junior multi-event athletes and the weather beat him. It was perfect for the week spent preparing in the university town on the Canadian prairies. The Province's Premier was on the verge of declaring a drought because of the long, dry spell but the weekend of the competition made it unnecessary. A strong wind blew on the first day and brought in rain on the second. Thompson, remarkably, scored 4505 in the first five events but never stood a chance of improving a single personal best on the second day. So bad were the conditions by mid-day that the pole vault was switched indoors to the field house of the university. Finally, he ran a single stride of the 1500 metres to validate his score of 7936 points for the team's sake, and pulled up. It won him the individual competition, and Britain the match. The BAAB could not have asked for more.

CHAPTER NINE 1982

To size up Jurgen Hingsen, you take the guided tour. One awesome dimension much quoted is his height; whether it is as 2.04 metres or 6 feet 7 inches, it gives you a crick in the neck. It is only the half of him. High jumpers are tall and you could fit two in Hingsen's frame. The Germans must have borrowed Goliath's cast to make him.

Thompson has been hurling small boulders at this giant with great effect for years. When Hingsen fell again to him at the Los Angeles Olympics, the score stood at Goliath 0, David 7. 'He's massive,' says Thompson, more with envy than admiration. 'His body and my speed … wouldn't that be interesting?'

66 1982 was a really good year for me. I tend to have a couple of good years then one easy year and so on. It was good to be back in competition at the European and Commonwealth Games, having taken things easy the previous year. I didn't like having to travel so far for the Commonwealth Games though — it was in Brisbane, a very long way away. For some reason only five or six of us fellows travelled with over one hundred and fifty girls and the rest of the men's team travelled separately. As luck would have it I was caught out by a strippergram. I was really embarrassed. It wouldn't have been so bad in front of just men, but one hundred and fifty girls really managed to make me look stupid! 99

They have been friendly without being friends for years, before Hingsen was a decathlete. Their first meeting was in a junior international match between Britain and West Germany in Bremen in 1976 when they were long jumping. Thomspon beat him in that also but, as fate would have it, struck up a long conversation with 'this long, thin guy'. Hingsen's talk was of becoming a decathlete and that gave them something to toss about while they waited their turns to jump. Next year, when they met at the European Junior Championships, he was a decathlete which rather meant that they were not talking anymore. Thompson was first, Hingsen third, and there was only 123 points between them. It was the closest the German came to him for another six years, and he has never finished within 100 points of Thompson.

Yet since Kratschmer's decline from the paramount place among West German decathletes, Hingsen has assumed his role as 'the rival', the effigy into which Thompson can stick the mental pins

which stimulate him to work so hard. 'When it's hurting bad, I tell myself it's all because of the boys in Germany and by the time I get to the competition all I want to do is take it out on them.' It was 1982 when Thompson first put Hingsen's face to it.

They have since met on training holidays, appeared together in chat shows and dined together. 'I decided at Christmas that he was a nice guy, yes, a good guy. We're a lot friendlier than the popular image of our rivalry because we've a lot more in common than most people. I respect him as a decathlete. He's good. But friends? How could we be? It's important not to be when you are after the same thing.

'He strikes me as being a bit arrogant but then I probably strike him as being incredibly arrogant. When we're on these German chat shows, he's always making these snide remarks, getting at me with little digs. But it's all in fun, all part of the show. At least I think it is.'

The rivalry had its origins in the summer of 1982. Thompson made his fourth visit to Gotzis, a warm-up for the European Championships and Commonwealth Games which were to follow. In the winter he had set a world best for an indoor pentathlon (five events) in Amarillo in Texas which featured a personal best in the high jump of 2.14 metres but there was nothing among his individual performances in early May to warn of what was to come. Not that too many people were wondering. At home he was becoming an anonymous athlete. The previous year had been one when Seb Coe and Steve Ovett were breaking world middle-distance records. The talk was of nothing else.

A moment's reflection in Gotzis.

'I wouldn't expect anything else,' said Thompson at the time. 'The boys have been going so well it was natural to forget a guy who is far away training for so long.' He was flattered that this time Fleet Street chose to follow him to Austria. 'It's nice of you people to show an interest,' was his greeting. 'Thanks for coming.'

He made it worth their while. On the first day he scored a world best of 4629. His shot and high jump were good and his 400 metres was outstanding, a personal best of 46.86 sec. Curiously, he did not sleep well that night but in the morning he was bursting to start. He ran a personal best of 14.31 sec in the hurdles into a headwind and his discus throw was his best in any decathlon. The pole vault was less than he expected and the javelin his poorest since 1978 but coming into the 1500 metres he needed only 530 points to surpass Kratschmer's record, hardly more than he scored with his trundling run in Moscow.

He achieved it with enough to spare to break the record by 58 points with a score of 8707, and such was his mood that evening that he gave a press conference in his hotel, tackling questions ranging across the spectrum from girlfriends and money to Coe and Ovett. 'I'm better at my event than they are at theirs because they have rivals very close to them and nobody can get close to me.' Fate did not waste time rapping his knuckles for the arrogance.

Hingsen was in the next room at the Gotzis hotel when Thompson was speaking to the British Press, relaxing with his American girlfriend. He had finished second that afternoon with a score of 8529 which was his best but unnoticed behind a world record. Two months later he scored 8720, 16 more than Thompson's record. 'It's not my exclusive property,' said Thompson but he was clearly shocked. 'I'd never considered him a rival. In many ways it came out of the blue for me. I was surprised he broke my record and I was even more surprised when he kept on doing it. If the first one was a surprise, the last couple have been baffling. I don't know where he gets it from.'

The German Press were ecstatic. Decathlon has a greater tradition in their country. They have had previous world record holders, and appreciate its significance. To have one again, and only three weeks before the European Championships, was a time for rejoicing. *Stern* magazine pictured their golden boy painted gold. 'Should have been silver, shouldn't it?' said Thompson cheekily.

Hingsen was not alone in threatening Thompson's ambitions for the European Championships. A second German Siegfried Wentz had also finished ahead of Kratschmer in this all-German competition. Thompson remembered him from Flein. He had introduced himself as 'the man who was going to break 9000 points first'. Thompson

In the tunnel entrance to the ancient stadium at Olympia

European Championships, 1982

offers the opinion that Wentz has no bad events. 'No outstanding ones either but that makes for a good decathlete. Still, it's not the same as being the best.'

Hingsen travelled with his retinue to Athens for the Europeans, his mother, father, his girlfriend and his coach. They checked in together to a smart hotel near the Parthenon, shared ironically, with most of the British Press. Thompson preferred a cooler, more rural retreat with the British team, sharing a room with Slaney 'which was good because we knew each other and that was good because it was going to be tough. They are all tough, however well prepared you are, but that was real tough.'

The confrontation between the two was exciting interest. The question most often asked was the effect on Hingsen of his world record. 'Shouldn't be a problem,' thought Thompson. 'Not physically anyway. Maybe mentally because he has come off a high and now has to climb back. But then with the European Championships coming up, he shouldn't have been getting on too much of a high three weeks earlier. That was up to him. In physical energy terms, it shouldn't be a problem.'

Thompson's only problem that summer had been an injury suffered when his pole snapped a month after Gotzis, slashing his arm, which needed several stitches to repair. His forearm was in plaster for three weeks. First time he tried to vault again five weeks later he failed to clear a height, but before he left Athens he had entered four more vault competitions and had cleared heights in all.

World record attempt, 1982

'I was looking forward to Athens. Hingsen breaking the world record didn't make any difference. I was ready. Of course it didn't make me feel any more kindly towards him but I could use that to my advantage, tell myself that he owed me.'

It was hot in Athens, and humid. It was 33°C. in the new Olympic Stadium, a beautiful bowl the

Greeks had built with the 1996 Games in mind and were using for the first time. 'I never thought for a moment that anything other than winning was a possibility. But it was a good competition. Terrific. He was good. He's always good but that time he was chasing all the way.'

In fact, Hingsen was having to chase because Thompson was making the running. After two events, Thompson was 171 points ahead. Decathlon always gives the runner-jumper a start. Hingsen, the runner-thrower, came back in the shot but scored only 4 more than Thompson. There were 167 points separating them still.

The high jump was another matter. Hingsen was soaring; Thompson was struggling. It has never been one of his better events. His comparatively short legs do not help, but it is not lift-off but run-up which lets him down. 'Oh, that run-up! I should be a 2.20 jumper. I wasn't taught well, that's the real problem. Once in a while I get it right but I never know when that's going to happen. I don't do it enough to get a pattern; there's no consistency. Maybe I didn't listen when I was young. I've got the upwards and the inwards bits but my foot is always in the wrong place at take-off.' It was that day. He managed 2.03 only at the second attempt and failed all three at 2.06. Hingsen did not miss once before 2.12 and at a third attempt leapt 2.15. The lead was down to 66.

At the end of the first day Thompson stretched it a bit again by running 400 metres almost a second faster than Hingsen. He went to bed that night 114

66 I've already mentioned my love of music and basically I like songs and records with good lyrics. My tastes are wide-ranging, from simple classical stuff like the Planets and Fingal's Cave to Phil Collins, George Benson and the Commodores. I like anything that's good. When I was young I was a disco-man, all Funkadelic and Parliament etc. I actually met George Benson in the States and had a great time recently watching Phil Collins rehearse for a concert tour. I've also met Colin Welland who wrote *Chariots of Fire* — one of my all-time favourite films and a movie with a really great soundtrack. Listening to Holst takes me back to school assemblies — I really enjoyed school. I read quite a bit, mainly sports books and science fiction. Sci-fi writers see that in thirty years time we'll probably be able to turn sea-water into gold for example but before writing it down a good writer will do his research and homework. I also like to see how people's minds work and how they solve problems. **99**

JAVELIN

Javelin is another event the Greeks performed only as part of the multi-event pentathlon, originating obviously from military training for spear throwing. Distance was the only objective and it did not matter how the spear was thrown. That is how it was until the 1950s.

Then an ingenious Spaniard discovered the best method was to use a discus-style turn while holding the javelin behind its normal grip in a pre-soaped hand for easy release. It went a long way but sometimes it did not go where it was intended. So the rules were changed to ban that style and now it must be thrown over the shoulder with one hand holding it at the grip. Discus-style turns are not allowed.

Specialist javelin throwers became so proficient that the East German Uwe Hohn threw more than 100 metres, and so to protect the public and other competitors in the arena, javelins will be of a different design from 1986. It will certainly reduce distances for the specialists but decathletes, who in the main throw less than 70 metres, may not be seriously affected.

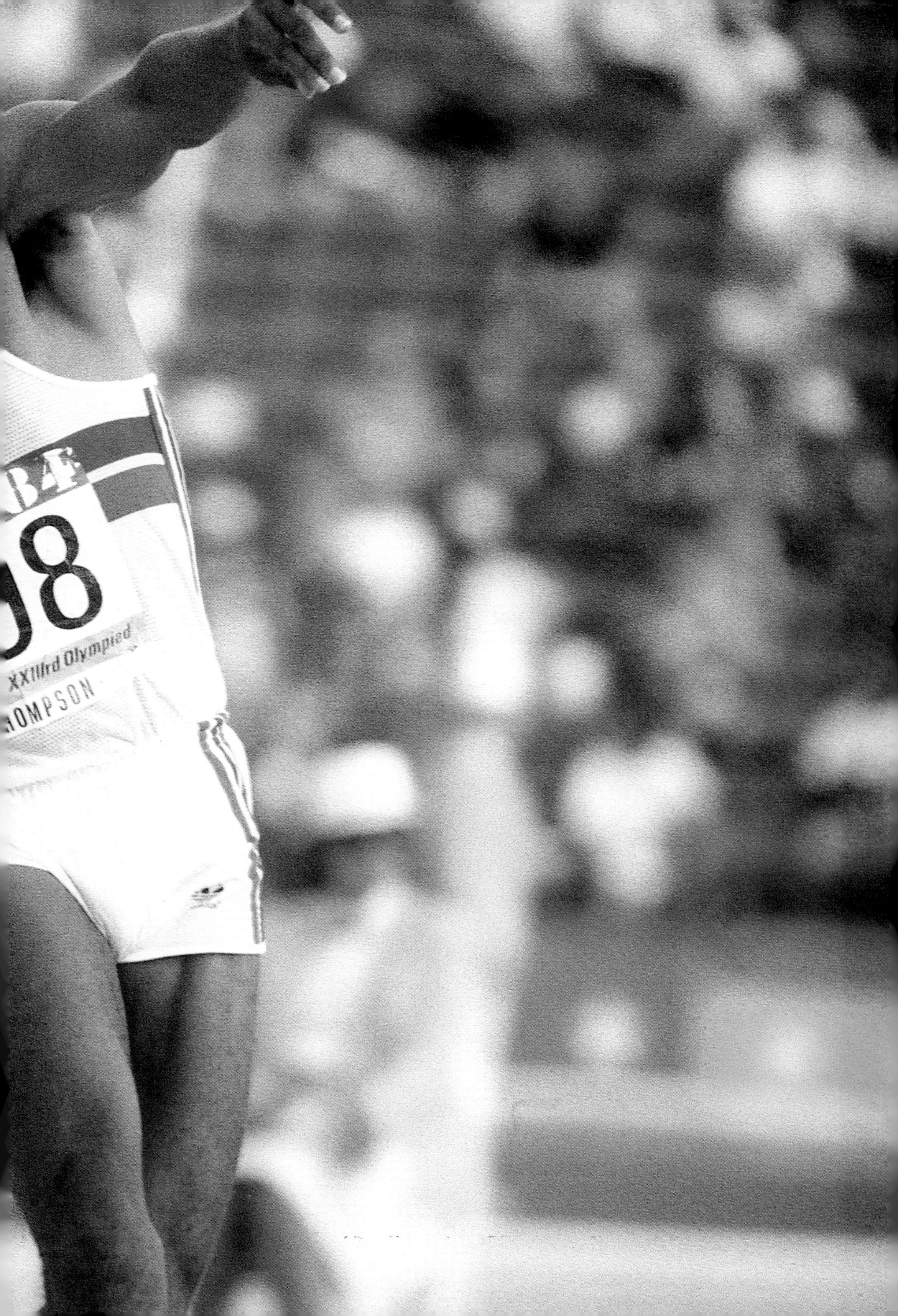

08
XXIIIrd Olympiad
HOMPSON

ahead. He doesn't remember how he slept. 'It isn't necessary to sleep, only to relax. I never remember being awake at four in the morning, even if I was, but. of course, you think about what happened. I should have done this, or that. I have done that. I was lucky here or that went well. I switch off between events during a competition but at night I run through it.'

The next day was September 8, a day that may live forever in athletics annals. Three world records and another European record fell within three hours. One was the decathlon. Thompson enjoyed that. 'It was nice. It didn't matter but it was nice. The others were really exciting. And Harold Schmidt's 400 metres hurdles I watched. Tremendous.'

Hingsen just could not hold him. A breeze which turned against Hingsen cost him dearly in the hurdles. His discus was unusually poor. His pole vault was lower than Thompson's. His javelin was his worst for three years. Thompson kept chipping away, building the lead until after nine events it was unassailable. He would have to break down in the 1500 metres to lose a lead of 237 points. But could he break Hingsen's world record?

66 The early '80s also saw me work on television for the first time. First in a magazine style series — 'White Light' with Gary Crowley and later on my own series for Chanel Four, 'The Body Shop', in which Dame Edna Everage, Roger Daltrey and Suzi Quatro among others appeared. I also saw that great movie *E.T.* and thoroughly enjoyed it. 99

World records do not often come in the major championship decathlons. The decathletes are tenser. There is more pressure. It matters. 'Doing technical events under pressure is so much harder. At Gotzis or somewhere like that, it's not a lot different from doing it in training, and how many athletes do you know who've said they've done better in training? All competition is harder than training but the "majors" are hardest of all. I don't go to the "majors" looking for a world record. I'd be happy winning with 7000 points if that's what it took in the particular circumstances. You can only do what the circumstances allow. Winning's what matters always.'

He had to run faster than 4 min 28 sec to pass Hingsen's record. The humidity and heat had drained him. His mind told him he had won anyway. But the occasion had got to him. World records had fallen. And suddenly there was Kratschmer getting into the act, pushing him, shouting, encouraging. The German was not in contention. He was far back, barely in the first ten, but he wanted his friend to have a go. Thompson could not distinguish his words but he got the message. Somewhere he found the energy. Together they passed one, then two men. They closed on Hingsen, Thompson ahead. He finished seventh in the race, the time 4 min 23.7 sec. The score was 8744, a new world record. He stood, hands on hips, catching his breath. Around him, Hingsen, Kratschmer and others lay exhausted.

"I'm on the 'phone to Ron's wife!"

'I would have gone down with them if they'd left any room,' he says. Finally, he found breath enough to stroll through a leisurely victory lap, wrapped in a Union Jack flag handed him from the crowd. Coe had lost the 800 metres final earlier. Ovett, injured, was commentating on the Championships for television. Thompson was the man of the moment,

feted. The fall was only around the corner.

He remained in Greece long enough to do some filming at Olympus for a friend's production company, before heading to Australia for the Commonwealth Games. He has never enjoyed flying, and suffers always from jet lag. He wanted to be there in good time to prepare himself for his first

defence of any title. If he won he would be the first to emulate long jumper Lynn Davies's achievement of holding Olympic, European and Commonwealth titles at one time. He arrived even before his England athletics team manager Andy Norman, and almost immediately landed himself in a storm of public criticism, whipped up by comments in newspapers at home, when he declined an invitation to carry the English flag in the opening ceremony.

That Thompson had not appeared in an opening parade since his first experience in Montreal in 1976 was forgotten. The reasons were ignored. Patriotism, my boy. Who was this young man to refuse the great honour? 'Patriotism, crap. What does England want — a flag carrier or a gold medallist? Who was it who was so stupid to think I would carry a flag for hours two days before my competition? Nobody even asked why I said no. They just got on their high horse about this patriotism thing. I couldn't believe it.'

The invitation had been a private matter. His declining it verbally, he considered, just as private. Why it was necessary for England's Games' officials to tell the world was beyond him. Why not only announce that Philip Hubble, the swimmer, would carry the flag, not that he would take the place of Thompson? 'I felt there was somebody there who didn't like it that there was this young, good looking black guy who enjoyed what he did. They were thinking of Empire and the Old School. They could not accept anybody who was his own man, who knew what he was. The critics had a great time with that one.'

He won the Commonwealth title anyway, not pushing himself more than was necessary. It was the first time he had scored fewer than 8500 points in a complete decathlon since Moscow and his lowest score since Prague. 'Disappointed? I'm always disappointed. Every time I go out I could always have done better. I'm not a perfectionist but I have such high expectations. But in Brisbane? It was enough.'

That winter he was awarded an MBE in the New Year's Honours List and an honorary degree by the University of Manchester. 'They gave the guy who invented the birth pill a degree at the same time. I thanked him for all the fun he'd given me.' He also thanked the athletics writers' and the sports writers' associations in Britain for making him their man of the year. 'I guess they had to. Coe and Ovett were injured,' he said.

"I think I had split my shorts and I was trying to find some privacy in which to change"

You have never read of Thompson citing injury as an excuse for any performance. He has been well enough to compete to his own satisfaction or he has not competed. It is not to say that he has never been injured, only that he has made it a policy never to talk about it. 'The public don't need to know because talking about it is only making excuses,' he says. 'All they need to know is that if I'm there doing it, it's because I'm fit enough to do it well.'

In 1983 there was a serious doubt whether he was ever well enough to do it well. Rumours circulated that Thompson was not healthy but since the man himself was never available to confirm or

> 66 As the years go by I train physically harder and am always trying to go faster, further and higher. I train seven days a week and at the end of the day I'm pretty tired but I never wish I was anyone else. If I miss a day's training I feel guilty and know I should have done it, I'm conscientious and unless I have a very good reason to I never miss a session. It seems unfair to train for years and miss days just for the hell of it and if I ever started to skip days I would realise my attitude had changed and that I might after all be getting bored. 99

deny it, the rumours never matured into anything. Those who knew anything kept it among themselves; those who did not know were those who did not need to know, like British officials, the Press and, most of all, those boys in Germany.

The troubles began for him in the winter in a long jump pit in an indoor hall in Toronto. The covering of sand was too shallow. Thompson jumped, landed and came out of the pit in a wheelchair. The shock flowed through his legs into his spine. There was a compression of the vertebrae. The X-rays which were taken showed up an older injury at the same site, possibly from that occasion before his first decathlon when he missed a pole vault landing bed. Thompson left Toronto for his winter training base in California on crutches.

'I was in real trouble. There wasn't much training I could do. Certainly not discus or pole vault, and whenever I ran for more than a couple of minutes my back would go into spasm. A bad back injury limits just about everything you want to do in training. I did nothing properly before halfway through May. The World Championships in Helsinki, Finland, were

then just twelve weeks away.

He needed, he felt, one competition before it. It would show him how much was lost and how much more must be done. Perversely, he chose Toronto again. An old friend, Andy Higgens, a multi-events coach and university lecturer there, arranged a place for him in the Canadian Championships, not an event ever noticed by North America's media. He travelled to it after barely a month's normal training. It was early June.

The wind in the Etobicoke Stadium was the only serious competition. It blew him to a quick 100 metres but nothing could disguise his anxiety about long jumping. The run-up was old, its rubberized surface lifting from the concrete and curling at its edges. The pit was well filled but short and before Thompson jumped officials dug out an extra metre of turf to lengthen it. His best was only 7.63 metres but even so his landing bounced him in another hop onto the surrounding track.

The gusting wind slowed his 400 metres and was so strong for hurdles that it would have ruled out any performance as a record had Thompson been trying for one. Again in the discus his lack of preparation was obvious, two fouls and a best of barely 42 metres, but in the vault he cleared 5.10. All was not lost but he fouled twice again in the javelin and, surprisingly, bothered to complete the 1500 metres for a final score of 8509.

A year later, at a similar period before the Olympics, Thompson was to test his progress again at a competition organised specially for him in Los Angeles. He was fitter than in Canada, and the BBC sent a special team to film it, but on that occasion he did not bother to start the 1500 metres. The difference lay in his expectations, not high for Toronto but considerable in LA a year later when he was fit and healthy. 'Sure, I should have finished but again all I was going to get out of it was another 8500 score and I'd done those too often. I was fed up with it. I didn't feel I had to do it because TV was there, any more than I felt I had had to do it for anyone else in Toronto. It was just how I felt. There's nobody in the world I have to justify not finishing to. Yes, one. Me. Not to Joe Public out there; we all know who he'll be putting his money on come the day.'

The money would have stayed in Joe's pocket were he to have known that within two weeks of Thompson arriving back in England, he was back on crutches; but nobody outside his small circle knew. For four weeks while Thompson fought to save his chances of going to Helsinki, it was a closely guarded secret. Not even British team officials were told.

It happened in a clothing shop in Crawley. The floor was newly washed. Thompson took a step, and did the splits. He hobbled from the shop.

Examination showed that he had torn his abductor muscle, pulling it almost off the bone. Training was out of the question, certainly any that involved the lower body. Most of the time he was too busy anyway getting treatment. Twice a day he drove to Guildford to see physiotherapist John Allen, a former hurdler himself who coached sprints, but the recovery was slow and time was running out.

'Finally, he took me to see this specialist who decided I would have to have an injection. When he took out this giant tube that looked more like a bicycle pump, your hero turned into the coward. I told him I'd rather retire then and there. No way was I having that in me, especially when he said if it doesn't work first time, he would try again. I fled.

'It was so frustrating. I had hardly had an injury in my life and in one year two stupid injuries that were crippling. Six weeks before a world championship and I was a hobbling cripple. In the end, of course, I was going to have to decide whether I would go to Helsinki. I was not taking anyone esle's place, so I could leave the decision late but it had to be worthwhile getting on the plane.'

So Thompson set a Sunday for a session at Haringey. He had not hurdled for six weeks but the other boys decided that he had to try it sometime. 'My groin was just sore now, not a sharp pain. Anyway four of us lined up and at the first hurdle, I fell flat on my face, I just couldn't get over it. We left it another twenty minutes and that time I fell at the second. It was crazy. It really looked bad for me.

'Then Greg came over and said ever so casual like: "Ah, you'll be alright. Save it for Helsinki". I died laughing. Here was a great champion who couldn't get over hurdles two weeks before the World Championships, and we were joking. I couldn't believe it was happening.'

It was around now that Thompson brought chief national coach Frank Dick into the picture. He would go to Helsinki and make a final decision as late as possible but no publicity. Nobody must know, least of all Hingsen. 'Why give him any encouragement?' Thompson took a plane before the rest of the team. 'I hardly wanted pictures of me hobbling onto a plane, did I?' In Helsinki, he kept out of the official Village, staying with Amercian sprinter friend Marti Krules who had rented a house for the summer there. He would go to the Village only to train, and then he would use a track well away from the others.

To pass the time he agreed to the *Daily Mail* organising a fishing trip for him in return for photographs of it. The other newspapers with photographers there were less than pleased. The next day they went looking for him. Perhaps he would pose some pictures for them. They tracked him down to his remote training track. 'And what do I do but fall over at a hurdle. I thought that's it, everybody

will know but they didn't know enough about it to realise I would never normally do that in training.' Before he tried again, Thompson asked security guards to send the photographers away. It seemed to them rude, arrogant and typical of him. Hingsen was posing for pictures and giving interviews, even putting his time at the disposal of British papers. What was wrong with Thompson's attitude? He couldn't and wouldn't explain. 'I didn't need a good press. Let them think what they wanted. The competition was the only thing that mattered.'

> 66 I really like shot, discus, javelin and pole-vault training. I enjoy all the feelings and get 'positive feedback' especially when I clear the bar! Infrequently I achieve personal bests in training but it is competition nerves which really drive me on. If I achieve a personal best in training I know I can do it again when it counts. Of course training sessions allow you to have a go time and time again and after 30 or 40 throws at the shot and discus, anything's possible. If a competitor is training harder somewhere I think "good for him". I try not to let outside influences affect me and I'm not stupid enough to think I train the hardest. 99

He had made up his own mind to start. Only Dick knew it but he was going to give the 100 metres and long jump everything and see what happened. 'I would give it 110 per cent. If it went, so be it, but if I could get through the first two, I reckoned I could handle it. They are the hardest on an injury and the ones I need most.' Thompson had avoided even the British team physiotherapist in case word got out, and accepted help only from a Finn unconnected with the championship organisation.

The leg was hurting still the first morning, and was not good throughout the competition, a dull soreness at the top of the left leg, but Thompson had a fair idea of what he could do with it in that shape. 'Marti and I sat down the night before and wrote a list of what I though I could do and what I thought Jurgen Hingsen could do, and it was going to be touch and go. In the 400 metres I figured I could afford for him to win by no more than a second, for instance, and actually he did it only four-hundredths of a second quicker.'

The weather befriended Thompson that day. It was not at its best, and a wind was swirling in the Olympic Stadium. Thompson's 100 metres was not good, only 10.60, but nobody else was better and the worst that could be said was that he had not had his usual great start to a competition. Again in the long jump he was down on his best and Hingsen was close but there was 114 points between them. Thompson knew he must go all the way.

From the stands, Thompson appeared to be enjoying it. He was smiling, bouncy, chatting to

people. Hingsen, as always, looked tight, unbending. The picture of a Prussian guardsman. It was just their different approaches. 'People say I'm trying to psyche him out, making light of it. I don't. I never smile to make him or anybody else feel bad. I'm enjoying myself. Why shouldn't I show it? This is what I like doing best. I might think to myself, "If I have a good throw here, it'll psyche him out", but never should I look at him or walk past him or get up when he's about to vault or something. Jurgen's attitude to me is never the same. In Helsinki when I came across him in the Village and said, "How are you, buddy", he gave me the cold look and turned his back. He keeps trying these different ways, finding out whether I'll crack. Keep on trying, Jurgen! I certainly don't intentionally try to psyche him out. I just go the best prepared I can to do the best I can, and if that influences others' mental states, it's not the main reason I do it.'

The apparent casualness in a competition is deliberate. He learned from watching men such as Jenner that total, unbending concentration for two days is not possible. In the heat of competition, a man can concentrate only in small doses. 'Physically, two days shouldn't be too hard. You're only throwing three times, jumping maybe three times and running everything once, and you do them all fifteen, twenty times every day in training. It's the mental energy that is different in competition.

'Chatting around is my way of breaking up the concentration. I go away from each performance, and let the concentration relax. I have seen pictures

"I reall
am a n
alone..

of me in the middle of a decathlon talking to people, or looking around or smiling but my eyes are alert, darting everywhere. I can turn it on and off. Try to keep it on for two days and it will slip when you don't want it to.'

It helps him greatly that Britain now has other decathletes good enough for major championships. They are people he can talk to, who speak the same language. There were none in Helsinki but an American friend, John Crist, was. In the Europeans the year before, an event in which the only English speakers were Britons, there was the Belfast athlete Colin Boreham and in Los Angeles there would be Brad McStravick. Daley still thinks that he might have won in Prague had he had Zeni there with him in the arena. 'It's difficult when you are stuck out there for two days with thirty people who don't speak your language.'

Helsinki was Hingsen's turn to have a bad high jump but he beat Thompson in the shot and 400 metres, though not by significant margins. Day one

left Thompson well down on his best score but Hingsen not much better placed than in Athens.

On the second day in the hurdles, he beat Thompson for a third time but again Thompson made sure it was too close to matter. In the discus, surprisingly, Thompson shaded it and in spite of Hingsen's best efforts he was second behind Thompson in the vault. He clawed back 26 points in the javelin but what was left for him was an impossible task — a time for 1500 metres at least 24 seconds faster than Thompson.

'Because I try so hard in the other nine events, almost all my inclination and resolve is gone by the 1500 metres. I am knackered mentally. I have been trying so hard I don't have much "try hard" left.

'That's why sometimes I'll go on in the pole

1500 METRES

The last of the decathlon's ten events ... and the least loved. It comes at the end of two days when he is at his most tired, and it is a rare decathlete whose physique is suited to it. The world record has been slashed in the last few years by specialist middle-distance runners but decathletes are usually content with times 50 seconds slower.

Daley describes himself as looking like a sprinter trying to jog. He calculates the margin by which he can afford to be beaten by his nearest rival in the competition and runs no faster than is necessary to keep to it. 'The event doesn't frighten me,' says Daley. 'I could do it but only if I needed to.'

In the last year he has been running in training three times a week, covering about four miles at 7-minute mile pace. It will not sound much to a specialist middle-distance runner but none of them have to carry 14 stone in weight.

107

"Everybody said what a great shot this was....the only reason I'm standing is because I can't find any space to lay down"

vault after all the others are out. Okay, so I'm enjoying it. How often do I get a large crowd and television watching me? But it's not that. I give 110 per cent to the first nine events. Some decathletes conserve themselves for the 1500 metres. My attitude is to put 110 per cent into nine so I know I don't need 100 per cent in the tenth.

'I run it like a sprinter. I know that. I don't look very good. I am not a 1500 metre runner. They weigh half what I do, and they run more often.

'I went out running with some of them in Edmonton. Supposed to be for four or five miles. We got lost and ended up doing eight. I stopped running for four years after that.

'So I do what's necessary. I count … like when I am behind Hingsen, I'll pick a point he passes and I count … one, two, three, four until I reach the same point. Then I know what I have to do, and I calculate.

He needs to beat me by 20 seconds, and it's 15, so I quicken up a bit.'

Thompson finished just over 8 seconds behind him in Helsinki. He was the world champion by a margin of 105 points with a score of 8555. Hingsen was second again, Wentz third.

'Not long ago, Jurgen said to me that if we ever got to the point where he has to beat me by 10 seconds, "I'm going to get you". Since that day I haven't missed a day's training. It inspired me. I run three times a week, perhaps four miles at seven-minute mile pace.

'Who knows what I can do at 1500? It doesn't frighten me. One day 9000 points will be there staring me in the face, and all it'll need is a 4 min 12 sec 1500, and I'll go for it. Just you wait, in the end all I can do is try …'

"This was taken during filming of the Lucozade commercial and it's Bruce, the director , explaining what the shot is going to look like"

CHAPTER ELEVEN 1985 & BEYOND

What Thompson would choose to do for an encore when he had won everything was not something which exercised his mind for long. He would do it all again but better, better than the first time or the second, better than anybody had ever done it.

So finding him in the Southern Californian beach resort of Capistrano Beach in February of 1986 came as no surprise. This was the final furlong of the run-in and to the Commonwealth Games and European Championships, Thompson was going about it in time-proven fashion.

Nothing had changed. Marti Krulee was there again, sharing accommodation and the training. The house itself, a two-bedroomed chalet standing on the pebble beach, was the same the two of them used for Olympic preparations in the winter of 1983-1984. Again they were making the daily drive each morning north to the track at the University of Irvine.

Yet, for all that, there was a difference, and not only that Greg was there filling one of the spare beds. Los Angeles was a watershed for Thompson. If Moscow was the end of the beginning, the period when the prodigy was growing to fulfil his potential, Los Angeles was the moment of his acceptance as a great champion.

He was Olympic champion for a second time, something only one other decathlete had ever achieved. He was Commonwealth champion for a second time, was current world and European champion and three times a world record breaker, a man unbeaten in nine completed decathlons since 1978. There was nothing left for him to prove.

After LA, Thompson was on the homeward run. He could call a halt to it at any time now and history would not judge him less generously. A few more

wins were not reason enough for driving himself forward day after day through exercises, drills and work-outs as stimulating after ten years as spot welding.

It was easy enough to say it was Hingsen still and 'the boys in Germany' and when it was cold, or he was tired, or it was hurting bad, he would use them to persuade himself to do it one more time, 'because I tell myself I'm doing it and maybe they aren't'. But that was a ploy, no more; had it been a purpose in life Thompson could have wound it up in 1984 and put Hingsen on his mantelpiece.

No, what was driving Thompson now on the inward-half was something more personal than pots and medals, something less tangible than victory over a certain man. Simply, it was pride. He wanted to be remembered, sure, and remembered as the best there ever was, but more than that he wanted to finish satisfied that he could have done no more.

On Capistrano Beach there was time to think, to ponder on how far his techniques had improved since LA, and how much more he could improve them before they were as good as they could be. He would not finish before Seoul in 1988, but he was certain now of when he would be ready to finish.

> 66 I'm also really interested in cars, especially fast or classic models. I was brought up in an age when everyone at four years old wanted an E-type Jag. My taste has changed now and my favourite cars include the Porsche 930 Turbo, Aston Martin Vantage, Masserati Bora, Porshe 959 and the Ferrari Daytona. I'm not really into the older shapes, I prefer streamlined vehicles. 99

With Hingsen, L.A., 1984

113

It would be a day like Jenner had in the Olympic Games in Montreal, a day when a decathlete finally puts it together. Not a personal best here and there, or even another best score for a world record. The whole thing, together, in one decathlon. 'You could walk away from it then. You'd have to. To do it just once would be all you could hope for. Whatever I've done so far, I've never got it together. Oh, yes, I'm proficient at everything, although there is room still for improvement. My personal bests now add up to more than 9000. It's getting it together that matters, making the sum total equal the sum of the parts. I haven't done that yet. That would be the best way to finish but there are too many ineradicable variables — weather, wind, rain etc.'

9000 points is not any more important to him than 8000 or any of the improvements were. It is another frontier but not the end of the journey. Its importance lies in being there first, in winning the race, but it will not stop there any more than the mile did with Bannister's feat.

He feels that he was as good as there in Los Angeles in 1984. 'Look at it like this: I ran 10.44 for the 100 metres into a headwind of 1.4 metres per second. Had there been no wind, it would have been 10.34 and the other round maybe 10.2 something. That's talking about an extra 50 points already. That would have put my final score on 8900 just because of a bit of wind, nothing to do with better training or technique or more strength.

'So that leaves me needing only 100 more from the 1500 metres which is 4 min 20 sec instead of what I did, and I can do that standing on my head.

'None of that takes into account that I had an okay long jump and a lousy high jump. So how far does that put me ahead of 9000 if I had put it all together? I'm a 9000-point decathlete now just

66 Obviously I sometimes take a break from it all, but I don't really enjoy holidays all that much because I really enjoy what I do as a career. I've had some great times though — scuba diving in the Cayman Islands and sea-fishing in Mauritius. It was on the sea-fishing trip that I caught my biggest fish, a 59 kilo yellow-fin tuna. This fish took thirty-five minutes to land and after wrestling with it from our little old boat I had forearms like Popeye. Even on holiday I do sit-ups and circuits but my training is not as serious as usual. 99

"Steve tells me this is art"

"After three Olympics this is the first tracksuit worth keeping"

looking at my LA performance, and it's as satisfying knowing that as doing it.'

When he arrived in California he was a better all-round athlete than when he left it last in 1984. He was certain that his hurdles had improved enough for him to run 13.80 sec, which would be worth about another 50 points, and his discus and javelin were better and his high jump more consistent. What he had not done since 1984 was to try them together in a decathlon. For the first time since becoming a decathlete in 1975, a calendar year had passed without him starting a decathlon competition.

There were enough individual competitions, one or two for Beagles and he turned up as one of the relay squad at some international matches, without being chosen, ahead of the specialist sprinters. It was the quietest year competitively he had had and for a British public accustomed to the regular appearances of middle-distance men, it was baffling.

Those whose opinions Thompson respects have never pressured him to compete. 'Tony at Essex Beagles phones me about a once a month to ask how it's going. It's never, "Will you compete"? They know that providing I'm not elsewhere, I'll always turn out for the Beagles. I love competition. There is nothing I'd rather be doing. I couldn't ask for a better club. They've been wonderful.'

So why no decathlons? 'Something like the decathlon is only any good doing if you are going to do it better than you've ever done it because you can't do that many. It takes time to get it ready, not physically so much as mentally. I keep on training until I get it right mentally and then I compete. Last year I never felt ready.'

He did not begrudge himself the break from competitions. 'I look at the gap between decathlons as preparation time. As long as there is the light at the end of the tunnel, I don't mind going on training without competition for a year, even two. One year, after all, is only preparation for the next and they fly by. We're in the States already! It's almost time now to compete.'

There are no financial pressures on him. He has never been paid to contest a decathlon, and the little he may be offered to turn out in track meetings as a sprinter is not enough to influence his judgement on what is right for him competitively.

What he earns comes his way because of his sport but not from it. He has a contract with the sports equipment company Adidas. He has made two television commercials for Fabergé's product Brut and another four for the soft drink Lucozade. He has given his name to Britain's most successful computer game, Daley's Decathlon, which earns him royalties.

None of it takes much of his time. 'About six days a year of actual work,' he estimates. 'As long

> **"** Although I was training in the States I was very much left alone by the U.S. media which I liked. The Americans respect their athletes and are keen to see people succeed. However just before the Games, I remember a funny incident when *Time Life* magazine commissioned photographer Neil Lither to take some pictures of me. The idea was to have me standing between two guards at Windsor Castle holding my javelin as if it were a weapon. Two American ladies went past, they started laughing and then I heard one say: "I thought Richard Prior was a lot taller than that". Such is fame. **"**

as there is enough to pay the bills and fill the petrol tank, I'm okay. I don't like messing up my routine more often than necessary.

'About two months after I did the Lucozade commercial at the beginning of 1984, they came back talking of another. They only wanted another two and a half days of my time but the first I could offer them was May 1986. They settled for that.

'I wasn't being awkward. I just happen to prefer doing other things. I like a routine, training early, going to my office to make a few calls, a bit of lunch and then more training. I work best that way, and right now money isn't the most important thing.'

He has never seen decathlon as a career. 'When I started, career prospects for a decathlete were zero.' He is sad that there are many athletes who come into the sport now looking for the money. 'I hear kids talking about show contracts and making money when they've just started and done nothing. It's a shame. The heroes or role models of the past never used to think like that.

'The attitude to the sport's so different now. They call it progress but it's a shame. Sport is worth more than that.

'Not long ago we had a few people throwing races. There are some people now paid money because they are notorious rather than good athletes.

'Last year we even saw "player power" creeping into it with that race in Zürich when Greg Foster, the American, got disqualified for two false starts and the others threw a tantrum and said they would not run unless he was reinstated. That's just the first time. They'll be more.

'And all the time, we're getting races where the opposition is fixed to suit one guy, fixed so he doesn't have to exert himself to win. The sport isn't as competitive as it should be anymore.'

Thompson blames the honorary officials running

the sport as much as athletes. 'They are mis-managing it most of the time, selling out to television and entrepreneurs, giving us meets full of running and nothing else.'

He has written to Arthur McAllister, chairman of the Amateur Athletics Association's general committee, expressing his views but has little faith in officials presently running the sport getting it right. 'Committee men, not athletics men,' he says scathingly.

'It's like last year when Bill Evans, the former chairman of the British Board, was quoted as saying that the difference between what they were paying the top men and the rest was too great.

'Where does he get that knowledge? Was he ever an athlete? No. Was he ever in the business of putting on athletics meetings? No. How does he know what men like Cram and Coe are worth?

'Can't officials understand that unless Cram and Coe are paid what they are worth, they won't run in Britain, and if they don't run, television won't show the meetings and sponsors won't pay up. Men like Coe and Cram were why ITV and sponsors are paying out so much.

'They are not there because of a decathlete or a jumper or a thrower. What shot putter ever gained the sport a TV contract?

'Coe and Cram and Ovett have done a great job for my sport bringing £15 million from sponsors and TV. You can't take anything away from them just because a few guys who aren't so good think they should have more. Let them try on their own and see how many sponsors stay around.

'It's not being selfish. It's realistic. Just because they don't get much money won't stop people becoming shot putters or high jumpers or decathletes. If you are 6ft 6in and 220lb you don't have a choice. It's the beauty of athletics — that everybody from 5ft 3in to the heavyweight of 25 stone has a place. I don't believe officials should bow to television with meetings that have nothing but races. That's wrong.'

Thompson and Cram are firm friends. Both fostered dreams of making it as professional footballers, Thompson far more realistically. They play together in charity matches, and play golf together (I'm only interested in hitting the ball further than anybody else') and after the Olympics, they both went on a tour of China.

'We won't do that again. What a place! So many people. One day Crammie and I were out walking and everybody seemed to be going in the opposite direction. So to make it easier, we decided to go with the crowd and then we found everybody was walking that way as well.

'We had a terrible time. All they fed us was fungus and seaweed soup. I'd have killed for a plate of fish and chips. You've never seen hungrier people. We were living off Maltesers.

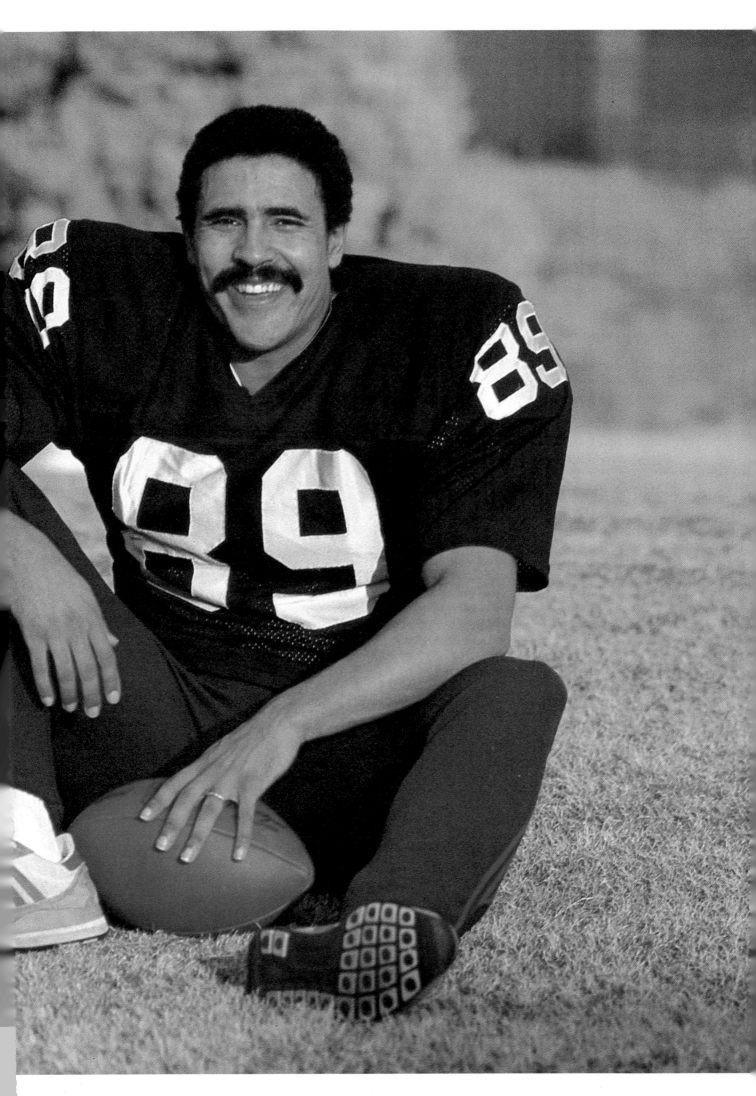

66 As usual I spent the year following LA, 1985, taking things easy. I enjoyed my home life and managed to buy a new house and get a compact disc player to listen to music on. I must have driven my new neighbours mad with the full-volume accompaniment to Leonard Bernstein's 'West Side Story'! Obviously I enjoy the trappings of success, but money isn't really important to me. I would still do what I do regardless. If I lost everything tomorrow, I wouldn't care as long as I could run. I live for athletics. Good athletes are very difficult people to cope with and especially live with. We are self-centred, self-opinionated and self-indulgent — to remain near the top of the tree you have to be. Single-mindedness is an asset. Anyone thinking about living with an athlete has to bear in mind the washing bin's always full of kit and the bedroom covered in athletic equipment — I probably have more sports shoes than the average family with six kids! **99**

'We turned up at one airport and found we had tickets to a place where the airport wasn't going to be built until 1990! We had a five hour journey on a train with wooden seats because of that.'

Thompson's popularity survives perversely the sniping of his critics and his long absences. When the London newspaper *The Standard* conducted a massive poll in association with a brewery, Thompson was voted the greatest of all athletes by a margin of 9000 votes from Coe and Roger Bannister, two of the middle-distance heroes.

What he envies the runners is the popular understanding of their events. It is a constant irritation that he is known for who he is but not for what he does. 'Daley Thompson, the 1984 pentathlon champion' was a caption under a picture of him in *The Sunday Times* this year.

He made it a condition of an interview with one famous ex-sportsman who writes about athletics that he name the ten decathlon events in order. 'He didn't know the ten, let alone the order,' he recalls. He did not get the interview.

'What's the point of giving an interview to a man who hasn't done the basic homework? It's like press conferences after the major championships. All I ever get asked is what happened in the competition which they are supposed to have just watched.

Outside Paramount Pictures

They never ask interesting questions.'

Sometimes they prove him wrong and he puts on a show for the Press. He did it in San Diego before the 1984 Olympics. 'The Daley Thompson Laugh-In' one Californian paper called it.

'All this talk of Hingsen is giving me a headache,' he quipped pulling off his baseball cap to reveal a bandage. 'Jurgen's promised the German people he'll bring back the gold medal. There are only two ways he can do that — steal mine or do another event.'

Other times the flippancy backfires. Like after the LA victory when a London news reporter asked at the press conference what Princess Anne had said to him when she approached him at the end of his victory lap. He joked that she had remarked upon his good looks. 'They were being nosey, and I was trying to tell them in a jokey sort of way to mind their own business. They didn't realise I was joking.'

When he remarked a few moments later that it was one of his ambitions to become a father, he was asked the identity of the lucky lady and what she had to say about it. He replied: 'I think you've already mentioned the lady, and she said, "I hope they're white".'

The Americans took it as a joke. 'Sir Daley of the decathlon is the male version of Joan Rivers,' said the *LA Herald Examiner*.

The Press Association, the news agency which represents all British papers, chose to edit the remarks themselves, not mentioning those which might have referred to Princess Anne. They put them out in full later without comment after critical comments in London's *Standard*. Other comment was uniformly critical at home.

Princess Anne jumped to his defence. Her press secretary Michael Shea issued an immediate statement dismissing it as 'totally absurd that anyone should think anything Daley Thompson said was offensive in any way'.

Chris Palmer, chairman of the British Olympic Association, observed astutely: 'These remarks are to some extent Daley's way of telling the Press to mind their own business. The Princess herself, who had chosen to greet Daley at the trackside in her capacity as president of the BOA, went further later. 'The media made me laugh because it was being so po-faced,' she said. 'Daley has got a perfectly good sense of humour, so you can't really take umbrage at it.'

66 I don't really think of the future too much. To do something like decathlon is all consuming. Probably 50,000,000 people in the world wish to be the best in athletics. The stop watch is your judge and you cannot cheat or think of something else for 25 per cent of the time because all the others will soon catch up. If at the end of the day no-one remembers what I did, I won't care as I know I got everything else out of myself and that I had done a good job. I wouldn't change anything at all except perhaps my position in the 1976 Olympics because I would like to have come first.

I'm looking forward to my fourth Olympic games: 1988 will be a tough Olympics. It will mean that I've been competing at the highest level of my sport for over 12 years. Bruce Jenner was at the top for only 4. My main aim for 1988 is to polish up my decathlon — to me it is one not ten events, and the key is constant training and dedication, not just harder and harder training. The whole point of training is to eliminate the need to rely on luck. 99

In the image, the sign reads: NEVER TRY TO TEACH A PIG TO SING IT WASTES YOUR TIME AND ANNOYS THE PIG

66 In future perhaps I will do more work in television. I'm already about to start work on my new American series 'Copper'. The screen test was good fun and the series is about an English copper new to the Los Angeles Police Department. Obviously I'm wary of being typecast in the traditional athlete mould of commentator, but if you've got a lot of inside knowledge then you've got to make money. Once I've done everything I'll be happy to step down and I'll try anything but real work! Once in a while though I realise that time is passing and in athletics you do live an accelerated pace. One day I will have to hang up my spikes but I'll still train two or three times a week and I will always stay fit. I haven't enough patience to be a coach, very rarely do good athletes make good coaches and I can't see myself trying to inspire thousands of people. I have very few regrets. Perhaps I would have liked to do gymnastics at school because I'm not naturally very supple and I would like to learn another language. I would like to see more youngsters try various multi-events out rather than specializing

Daley saw the questions as just another intrusion. 'I could have told them to piss off. They'd have expected that from me. Instead I turned it into a joke and they didn't see it.'

In fact, parenthood is a serious ambition of Thompson's. 'When I finish with decathlon, I'll want something else and I'll want to give it total commitment. I think being a good father would help fill the void.'

Finishing with the decathlon is not on the programme yet but it is on the horizon. He will be twenty-eight years old before he defends his European title in Stuttgart, and thirty before the 1988 Olympics. 'The other day I found my first grey hair.'

at an early age. Schools don't do a good enough job, but how can you teach athletics properly to thirty or forty people in a class in under an hour? It would be nice to see more youngsters consider decathlon but as always sprinting and running are the easiest things to practise and therefore develop. 〞

He will never leave athletics. 'I'd like to think the day I finish as an international athlete would be just the time I stopped training seven days a week, that I would still compete for my club, and do a few sessions with the boys. I'd still be around.'

What else could he do? 'Something will come up. As long as I perform as well as I can between now and when I retire, something will happen afterwards. Something's bound to come up. Always does.

'I'm lucky like that. Like in that biology exam.'

66 I would just like to be remembered as a good athlete — it's up to everyone else to make their own subjective opinions of me, but I think my qualifications stand up against anyone. It would be nice to be remembered as the greatest but it is in my own mind that I need to know that I've done well and fame in itself is not of the slightest importance. It's nice to know, however, that my success has allowed me to have bulk deliveries of Gummy Bears shipped over from the States to satisfy my sweet tooth. **99**

"This picture depicts my reaction to what was the best and worse moment of my lifetime. It was the final throw in the discus at Los Angeles. I'd had two pathetic throws and Hingsen had thrown exceptionally well and going into the last throw, everything was on the line and this I believe is the moment that any athlete looks forward to in a masochistic kind of way because this is the moment of truth, either you win or lose "